W9-CNR-485

"As a dad of five children—two of them born when I was 47 and 49—I heartily endorse this book. Beth Vogt offers just the right blend of personal experience and professional expertise to encourage and equip women to embrace their roles as later-in-life moms."

Dr. Kevin Leman, author,
Making Children Mind without Losing Yours

"Packed with practical tips, real-life stories, and helpful hints, *Baby Changes Everything* offers a look at motherhood from a slightly different perspective—through bifocals. It is a perfect blueprint to consult on your new adventure called 'mid-life mothering.'"

Jane Jarrell, author, *Simple Hospitality*

"What a gift! Beth Vogt has created a book that not only contains vital resource information for older moms but also stories from those who share in this late life, joyful journey. My only complaint is that this book was not around when I had my first child at 41 and my second at 43!"

Gail Hayes, author, speaker,
and proud AMA mom

"Beth Vogt uses humor, real-life stories, and facts to give us a warm but unvarnished journey into the joys of late-in-life motherhood. You will laugh out loud and learn all about the pressures of becoming a 'mature mommy' in today's world. An entertaining and educational read!"

Byron C. Calhoun, MD

BABY CHANGES EVERYTHING

Embracing

and Preparing

for Motherhood

After 35

Beth K. Vogt

Revell

Grand Rapids, Michigan

© 2007 by Beth K. Vogt

Published by Fleming H. Revell
a division of Baker Publishing Group
P.O. Box 6287, Grand Rapids, MI 49516-6287
www.revellbooks.com

Printed in the United States of America

All rights reserved. No part of this publication may be reproduced, stored in a retrieval system, or transmitted in any form or by any means—for example, electronic, photocopy, recording—without the prior written permission of the publisher. The only exception is brief quotations in printed reviews.

                    Library of Congress Cataloging-in-Publication Data
Vogt, Beth K.
    Baby changes everything : embracing and preparing for motherhood after 35
/ Beth K. Vogt.
        p.   cm.
    Includes bibliographical references.
    ISBN 10: 0-8007-3067-4 (pbk.)
    ISBN 978-0-8007-3067-3 (pbk.)
    1. Middle-aged mothers. 2. Motherhood. 3. Older parents. 4. Mother and
infant. I. Title.
HQ759.43.V64 2007
306.874′30844—dc22   2007010679

Scripture is taken from the HOLY BIBLE, NEW INTERNATIONAL VERSION®. NIV®. Copyright © 1973, 1978, 1984 by International Bible Society. Used by permission of Zondervan. All rights reserved.

In keeping with biblical principles of
creation stewardship, Baker Publishing Group advocates the responsible
use of our natural resources. As a
member of the Green Press Initiative,
our company uses recycled paper
when possible. The text paper of
this book is comprised of 30% post-
consumer waste.

green
press
INITIATIVE

To my husband Rob,
the words "I couldn't have done this without you"
have never been truer

To Josh, Katie Beth, and Amy,
who wholeheartedly love their youngest sister

And to Christa,
the reason I embraced late-in-life motherhood

Contents

Foreword

*M*ommy-come-lately is a term Beth Vogt coined to describe women who have children after the age of thirty-five. I am a mommy-come-lately, and perhaps you are too. All "mommies-come-lately" have unique stories; we also have a lot in common.

I remember vividly a morning six years ago when I was feeling particularly "unique." I was forty-one years old and three months pregnant with my first child. It suddenly occurred to me that while I had heard of older first-time mothers, I didn't know any personally. I didn't actually know anyone who'd been in my position! In spite of my excitement about the child we were expecting, this realization made me feel somewhat uncomfortable and a bit lonely. I would have loved to have been handed this book on that day.

In my case a combination of circumstances, including my husband Jack's chronic illness, led to this moment. Of course that was only on the surface—the stuff we could see. Underneath, as always, was the hand of God faithfully, intricately at work in our lives.

When I was married at twenty-six, my plan was to have the first of two children before the age of thirty. Around thirty-five I was complaining silently to God that the calendar of my life was running behind. I was not in control, and I was feeling frustrated and anxious. Of course, God hears our silent complaints. He patiently brought me through the process of embracing his will for even this part of life—whatever it might be.

I made peace with the possibility of never having children. But I didn't completely lose hope. At forty-one my prayer was not "God, please give us a child" but rather "Please do what you know is best for all concerned." Jack's health was significantly improved at this point, and I was busy writing an album of lullabies for other people's children. The fact that I was able to pour my whole heart into those songs felt like a victory to me. The entire writing process was filled with joy, and when I was finished I recorded the songs and sent them off to my producer.

Almost exactly one month later I found out I was pregnant. Talk about God being involved in our lives! He doesn't just love us. He goes to the most amazing lengths to make sure we know it!

Shortly after J.P. was born, I felt God saying to me, "Remember that calendar? I have one too, but mine is bigger and more accurate—and it never runs behind!" David said, "I trust in you, O LORD. . . . My times are in your hands" (Ps. 31:14–15). Maybe that's the best thing mommies-come-lately have in common: we understand that!

When I was pregnant, I prayed every day that God wouldn't let anything or anyone interfere with his perfect plan for this child. Now J.P. is six. Like all Christian parents, Jack and I already see God's hand at work in our son's life. And like all Christian parents, we pray that we will be godly examples and that we will always support and never interfere with God's plan.

We're homeschooling this year, and J.P. is surrounded by grandparents, uncles, aunts, an ever-growing number of cousins, and two adoring, grateful, and sometimes exhausted parents. (For a while after Jack's last birthday, J.P. delighted in bragging to everyone that his daddy was fifty!)

If you are a mommy- (or daddy-) come-lately, you'll find some wisdom and encouragement in this book. You'll also find a few friends who've been somewhere near where you are. Your times are in God's hands—and you are unique, but you are not alone.

Twila Paris

Acknowledgments

Some say that writing is a solo occupation. Not true. Many thanks to

Colleen, Gaylyn, Gloria, Linda, Scoti, and Sharon, members of my writing group, Inkspired, and my writing "duo" partner, Tiffany: without your insights—and cold-blooded critiques—I would never have written this book.

My family: home is where your story begins. In my heart, you all make up "home."

Everyone who shared their experiences with me: I am blessed to tell your stories. They are the heart of *Baby Changes Everything*.

Mary: thanks for going along for the wild ride of writing this book—and for being my friend.

My wonderful friends who were my "spiritual ground support" and prayed for me as I wrote this book: Chris, Dale,

Dianne, Faith, Fran, Jamie, Jean, Pamela, Renee, Roxanne, Susie.

Dr. Mark Campbell: I threw you so many curveballs during my late-in-life pregnancy. Then I pitched you the idea for *Mommy-Come-Lately*, and you were willing to be part of this too! May every mommy-come-lately find a medical provider as knowledgeable and compassionate as you.

Carmen Leal: thank you for your expert guidance. You are a brainstormer par excellence!

And to my other Beths:

Beth Jusino: we met across the conference table as editor and writer. Okay, I admit it—we met in the ladies' room at the Broadmoor Hotel. I am grateful we became friends. Thank you for listening to me hash out the idea for this book and for encouraging me to pursue it.

Beth Lagerborg: let's do this again sometime! Thank you for believing in me and for believing in this book.

Introduction

The oldest trees often bear the sweetest fruit.

German proverb

This book is an invitation. If I could, I'd inscribe your name on the dedication page and then write: embrace your life as a late-in-life mom. Be willing to let go of preconceived ideas about how your life would play out. Get ready to welcome your child—and expect to be changed by him or her.

If you are a pregnant woman age thirty-five or older, you know how the medical community labels us: Advanced Maternal Age (AMA). As far as I am concerned, those three words are just another way of saying I'm old.

So I'm replacing AMA with a new phrase: *mommy-come-lately*.

Let me explain. My term—*mommy-come-lately*—is closely related to the old term *Johnny-come-lately*. If you rush to look up that term in your dictionary, you may not even find it in newer versions of Merriam-Webster's. Not many people use it anymore. So what is it?

A Johnny-come-lately is someone who has only recently started a job or activity and has suddenly become very successful.

Put a maternal spin on that—late-in-life motherhood—and you now have a mommy-come-lately: an older, successful mom.

There are all types of mommies-come-lately:

women who chose to wait to have children while they pursued education and careers

women who were surprised by a late-in-life pregnancy

women who adopted children in their midthirties or forties

women who battled infertility or chronic illness to become pregnant

women who became mothers in their twenties—and continued having children into their forties

women who remarried and became a late-in-life mom in a blended family

I designate myself as a "repeater" mommy-come-lately. My fourth child was born twelve years after my third. My friend Mary is a "first-timer" whose only child was born when Mary was forty-six. I wrote this book for moms like Mary and me.

My childhood dream of writing a book was more along the lines of penning a great American novel. But writers are told to "write what you know," which means I write what I live. I'm not an expert on pregnancy and childbirth. But as a mom of four who's been where you are today, I can offer to you what I looked for during my own unexpected pregnancy: encouragement and practical advice. And that's what *Baby Changes Everything* is all about!

1

The Best-Laid Plans

The best-laid plans of mice and men often go awry.

Robert Burns, "To a Mouse"

Mary and I are opposites.

I am tall. Mary is petite.

I am hazel-eyed. Mary is blue-eyed.

I am a stay-at-home mom. Mary is a work-from-home mom.

I have four children. Mary has one.

Here—as mothers—is where our lives intersected in unexpected ways.

My youngest child Christa was born when I was forty-one—twelve years after my third child.

After years of infertility derailed her dreams for children, Mary's son Justin was born when she was forty-six.

A Funny Thing Happened on the Way to the Empty Nest

I designated my childbearing years to my twenties. Within the span of one decade, my three children—Josh, Katie Beth, and Amy—were born.

Mission accomplished.

Without a backward glance at morning sickness, labor and delivery, or breastfeeding, I lived life as a mom. While my hormones got back to normal again, my body lost its "baby weight" one last time.

My official role was to be my children's helper. I helped them master potty training, eating with a fork, picking up their dirty clothes, brushing their teeth, being kind to one another, and being obedient to me.

Along the way I learned things too. I discovered that, as my girlfriend Scoti says, mothering is a permanent state of exhaustion. A mom never clocks out. Keeping up with preschoolers demanded energy, creativity, and perseverance.

I surrounded myself with other parents who knew what they were doing. I traded parenting tips and read articles about teaching my children to share, excel at school, and resist peer pressure.

Occasionally the question popped up: why not one more child?

For one, my husband Rob felt challenged to be an involved and available dad while juggling the demands of his job as an Air Force physician. A fourth child could stretch him to his parental limit. I also watched my youngest sister struggle with infertility. Knowing her dream of motherhood eluded her, I just couldn't imagine saying, "I'm pregnant again." Besides, having babies was part of my twenties, not my thirties. I enjoyed watching my friends continue to have children. That was just not in the Vogt Family Plan.

Fast-forward twelve years.

Rob and I were parenting two teens and one preteen. Dinner conversations included topics like how to make right choices and what movies are acceptable and statements like "No, we are not buying you a new car when you get your driver's license."

I had not experienced the "baby wants" in years. To humor friends who questioned why we weren't having any more children, I attended a fall festival dressed — in all my padded glory — like an abundantly nine months pregnant mom-to-be.

"I'm done having children," I told my friends with a laugh. "This is the closest you'll ever get to seeing me as a pregnant woman."

A year later, my body was feeling out of sorts. Occasional mild bouts of nausea accompanied by more than I-live-with-three-teens tiredness. I was fast approaching my forty-first birthday. Was it time to read up on menopause? Before checking out a stack of library books, Rob and I decided to rule out the most obvious *im*possibility.

My physician husband dutifully carried my urine sample off to his medical clinic. His good-bye kiss was accompanied with the statement, "You are not pregnant."

I called him midmorning and asked, "So, when do we find out I'm not pregnant?"

Silence.

A long silence.

Rob was so shocked when he saw my results, he had trouble reading the computer screen. He double-checked my lab results, figuring he pulled up another woman's chart.

"What would you think if you *were* pregnant?"

Why was he asking me that?

"Am I pregnant?"

"Well, according to this you are."

Within seconds I was screaming and crying, overwhelmed with a you-have-got-to-be-kidding-me hysteria.

"Let me talk with Mark Campbell and see if he'll do an ultrasound to make sure you're pregnant," Rob suggested. Dr. Campbell was an obstetrician and a close friend. Rob didn't tell me that he was certain I was pregnant. He was just buying us some time to get used to the idea.

Early that afternoon I reclined on an examination table, my tummy slathered with cold, goopy gel. Dr. Campbell moved an ultrasound sensor back and forth. Rob and I watched the monitor—and saw a tiny beating heart.

Dr. Campbell looked in my eyes, smiled, and confirmed, "Congratulations, Mom."

Three days before turning forty-one, menopause wasn't looming on the horizon. Morning sickness and maternity clothes were. I was AMA—a pregnant woman of Advanced Maternal Age.

Knowing we couldn't hide our surprise, Rob and I decided to tell Josh, Katie Beth, and Amy right away. That evening as we enjoyed dessert at a local restaurant, Rob said, "I'm glad all six of us are here."

"Five, Dad," Josh corrected, giving Rob a quizzical look. His dad knew how to add!

"No. *Six*," Rob repeated.

Only a second or two passed before Josh looked at me and asked, "Are you pregnant?"

I managed to blurt out yes before bursting into tears.

Other than grinning, Josh, my introvert, didn't say much. The girls made up for his silence by shrieking and jumping up and down. The Vogts were having a baby.

My twin sister Brenda sent a birthday card to me via overnight mail. In it she wrote, "Thanks for proving that at forty-one anything is still possible!" A few months later she had her tubes tied.

A lot of people laughed when they heard our news. I was not laughing. I did not want to be pregnant. I told a friend that it felt like a cosmic joke—but my belief in God wouldn't let me designate my unexpected baby as some sort of hormonal prank.

"Now I know what an unwanted pregnancy feels like." I sobbed as I said those words to Rob. He knew not to try to reason with

The Mommy-Come-Lately Movement

Motherhood is experiencing an extreme makeover. Look in the mirrors of today's moms and you see women in their thirties and forties—not just the twentysomethings of generations past. The dominant birth rate trend of the last decade reveals an increase in AMA moms (those aged thirty-five years or older). For example, the 2002 birth rate

- was 31 percent higher than in 1990 for women thirty-five to thirty-nine years
- increased 51 percent from 1990 rates for women forty to forty-four years
- more than doubled from 1990 rates for women forty-five to forty-nine years[1]

A more recent study from the National Center for Health Statistics stated that births to older women continued to increase from 2004 to 2005. During that time, the birth rate

- increased 2 percent for women thirty-five to thirty-nine
- increased 2 percent for women forty to forty-four
- increased slightly for women forty-five to forty-nine, the highest rate for this group since 1970 (although this figure only reflects a small total number of births)[2]

1. Centers for Disease Control, "Birth Rate for Women Aged 40–44 Years Rose in 2003, New Report Finds," news release, November 23, 2004.
2. National Center for Health Statistics, "Births: Preliminary Data for 2005," CDC website.

a hysterical pregnant woman. Instead, he let me cry. As I did, I placed my hands over my tummy. "It's nothing personal, baby," I insisted. "It's not that I don't want you. I just don't want to be pregnant."

Hope Deferred

"I always wanted to have a large family—six kids," Mary said. From the time she was twelve years old, she babysat constantly. As a twentysomething single woman, she watched the children of moms her age who needed a night out.

Mary finished college and pursued a career in communications. "I realized I might get married later. But I never imagined I wouldn't be able to have kids," Mary recalled.

She was thirty-five years old when she married Doug, and they believed having children would happen easily. Mary's ob-gyn cautioned, though, that it might take longer for Mary to get pregnant because of her age. During six unsuccessful years, Mary endured people asking her why she wasn't having a baby. Finally she was referred to an infertility specialist, who then put both Mary and Doug through a battery of tests.

"The results were 'infertility, with cause undetermined'—despite the doctor telling me that my FSH hormone level was that of a person seven years younger," Mary said. "I thought for sure they'd find something wrong. When they didn't, I realized my options were limited by my age."

The specialist warned Mary she didn't have a lot of time left to pursue treatment. After talking and praying, Mary and Doug decided not to pursue other possible alternatives like in vitro fertilization or adoption.

"If it was meant to happen at our age, it would. Doug and I didn't want to go through the emotional roller coaster of treatments. If we'd been younger, maybe we would have."

With the door to motherhood closed, Mary grieved that they would never have an heir to carry on the family name. "We had no one to transfer our memories to. That was the hardest thing to deal with — it stopped with us. Just seeing another mother holding her baby made my heart ache because it reminded me of my barrenness.

"I always believed that if we were meant to have a child, God would work it out. I tried not to dwell on my disappointment. But slowly I gave up the dream of motherhood and began pursuing my master's degree. I couldn't change anything. I needed to move on."

Going to school and working full-time consumed all of Mary's thoughts and stopped her from sitting home and thinking about not having children.

Then, four years later, when Mary was forty-five years old, a routine Pap test came back abnormal, raising the fear she might have cancer. Her ob-gyn had closed her medical practice, so Mary consulted her infertility specialist instead. After further testing, he performed surgery to remove a uterine polyp. Despite years of disappointment, Mary requested he be careful and not cause any damage that could prevent pregnancy.

"My request was sort of irrational. I believed it was still possible for me to get pregnant — even though I was telling myself and others it would never happen."

> *Age does not define a person, and therefore, being a mother and being older doesn't define a person either.*
>
> Andrea, repeater mommy-come-lately at thirty-six, thirty-eight, forty, forty-two, and forty-three

Trendsetters: Famous Mommies-Come-Lately

Pregnancy is news these days—*big* news.

From women's magazines like *Good Housekeeping* and *Self* to *People*, the editorial spotlight is focused like a laser beam on pregnant women.

The concerns, risks, and experiences of mommies-come-lately have a prominent place in the limelight. Journalists write about *who* is pregnant and *how* they got pregnant and *what* they're doing and wearing while they are counting down to their due date. The American College of Obstetrics and Gynecology (ACOG) even publishes a magazine called *Plum*, written specifically for Advanced Maternal Age (AMA) moms and moms-to-be.

In short, the late-in-life motherhood trend is garnering attention—and it shows no sign of abating.

Newswomen Making News as Mommies-Come-Lately

Newswoman Joan Lunden graced the cover of the July 2005 *Good House-keeping* magazine. She cradled a pair of newborn twins while her then two-year-old twins stood beside her. You've got that right—*two* sets of twins. Lunden's three daughters from her first marriage were then seventeen, twenty-two, and twenty-five. When she remarried, Lunden first attempted in vitro fertilization (IVF) and then pursued surrogacy. Both sets of twins were carried by the same surrogate mother—who was herself a late-in-life mom! Lunden was fifty-two when the first set of twins—a boy and a girl—were born. The second set of twins—also a boy and a girl—were born when Lunden was fifty-four. That makes Lunden an Olympic caliber mommy-come-lately in my estimation!

Sue Herera, who coanchors CNBC's two-hour daily business show *Power Lunch*, became a first-time mom at forty-six after four years of IVF treatments. Herera became pregnant within a month after she and her husband learned an adoption agency had twin

Two months after the surgery, Mary missed her menstrual cycle for the first time in her life—and, also *for the first time in her life*, she wondered if she might be pregnant.

Mary figured her positive at-home pregnancy test couldn't possibly be true. But during a follow-up exam with her ob-gyn, she rejoiced at seeing the amazing black-and-white image of a tiny beating heart on the ultrasound screen.

girls available for them to adopt. Twelve weeks into her pregnancy, Herera began bleeding. Although an ultrasound showed she had miscarried, she was still pregnant. She had been pregnant with twins, and her baby boy was alive and healthy. Daniel was born just a few months after they adopted their daughters Jackie and Vickie.

Actresses Take Center Stage as Mommies-Come-Lately

Actresses are trendsetters—usually because of what they wear, what kind of designer purse they carry, or what makeup line they use. But these days actresses like Julia Roberts, Sharon Stone, Jane Seymour, Brooke Shields, and Geena Davis are part of the mommy-come-lately movement. Roberts was thirty-six when she gave birth to her twins, Hazel and Phinnaeus. Stone adopted her son, Roan, when she was forty-two years old. She then adopted two more sons, Laird and Quinn. Davis was forty-six when her first child was born and then gave birth to twin boys when she was forty-nine. Actress Jane Seymour gave birth to twin boys, Johnny and Kris, when she was forty-four years old.

What the News Is All About

Newspaper and magazine articles aren't just focusing on who is getting pregnant. Journalists also write about options like surrogate mothering, IVF, and adoption. Stories discuss the risks of being an older mom—and outline how to have a healthy AMA pregnancy.

The December/January 2006 issue of *Child* magazine published an article titled "The Promise—and Perils—of Genetic Testing." The article discussed the pregnancy of a thirty-six-year-old mom-to-be. In a 2005 *Glamour* magazine article titled "Are Women Doing Things in the Wrong Order?" two writers debated whether women should have kids first and career later or vice versa. And the latest—and hotly debated—news is about the Spanish woman who gave birth when she was sixty-seven.

A friend said it best: "Finally the woman who always loved everybody else's kids has her own child to love."

Company of Friends

Despite living two hours away from each other, Mary and I get together every couple of months. Sometimes we meet for a girls' lunch without our kids or do a couples' date with our husbands. Other times we choose outings that her son Justin and my daughter Christa enjoy.

Our conversations are interrupted as we follow Christa and Justin through a kids' museum or around a playground or a water park. I talk about my son's pursuit of a publishing career. Mary talks about meeting work-related deadlines. We discuss the school options available for Justin and Christa. At times we stop and just watch our two children playing. We marvel at how they have changed everything—us, our families, and our plans for the future.

The challenges of being a mommy-come-lately—a successful, older mom—are more easily faced in the company of friends.

When Mary faced a tight deadline, I spent the morning in a children's museum with Justin and Christa while she got her work done. Mary listens when I talk about the challenges of Rob's private medical practice. I listen when Mary tells me about her husband's campaign for sheriff. We both hope Justin's and Christa's plans to marry when they grow up come true. (Moms can dream, right?)

Even though our stories of how we came to late-in-life motherhood are different, we both treasure the unexpected blessing. And we're thankful we can walk this path of motherhood together.

The Bottom Line

If you're a mom, you get plenty of advice from family and friends—and sometimes from strangers you meet in the grocery store. You'll find some advice in this book too. But I'm not going to tell you how to read *Baby Changes Everything*. Read it front to back or back to front. Or glance over the table of contents to find the topics that apply to you right now. But no matter what, enjoy the experience and be encouraged by the knowledge that you're not alone on the mommy-come-lately path.

Cameo Appearance: **Alice**

Repeater mommy-come-lately by choice at thirty-five and again at almost thirty-seven

Husband: **Gary**

Children: **Megan, age twelve; Abby, age eleven; Matthew, age ten**

Alice was the first voice of MOPS (Mothers of Preschoolers) for me. When I called her about joining my church's MOPS group, I made sure she knew how old I was.

"Come on and join us!" Alice said. "I'm an older mom too."

Alice chose to have children when she was older. She says, "Couples need to trust their judgment and to do what they think is right when it comes to having children. I wasn't ready earlier to be a mom. I'm glad I waited.

"I was one of the many women who chose to first have their career, travel, go to college, and develop a secure relationship with my spouse."

When she finally started a family, Alice received mixed responses from people. "Some moms seemed to almost envy me for waiting," she says. "My husband, Gary, and I struggled less with finances. And some moms pitied me. It was like they said, 'Look! I'm free and you're just having yours!'"

Alice heard about MOPS through a Christian radio broadcast. She was attracted to the idea of connecting with other moms. But there was a waiting list for her church's MOPS group.

"My pastor's wife told me if I became a care group leader, I could be in MOPS. So I did, even while I was in the Air Force and working nights," Alice recalled. "At first I felt like a fish out of water. I had not been exposed much to women — just the wives of those I worked with. But as I got to know the other moms, I really liked them. They were a great change from my night job!"

Cameo Appearance: **Linda**

Mommy-come-lately by adoption at forty-seven

Husband: **Dave**

Daughter: **Tori, age twelve**

Linda admits that she had a heartbreaking journey to motherhood.

"I was the second oldest in my family. My older brother and I were the ones who took care of the younger children," Linda said. "I was not going to have any kids. I felt like I'd raised my brothers and sisters. I didn't want to be taking care of children anymore."

After dating for five years, Linda and Dave married. She was thirty-three and he was thirty-eight.

"I wanted my career. I wanted to be working. I had no desire to have children," Linda said.

Until she turned forty-five.

"Then we thought, 'We need to do something!' Our careers were no longer satisfying. I wondered, 'Why am I doing this? Where am I going with all this? I have nothing to show for my life.'"

Her physician warned Linda that because of her age, her chances of having a baby were slim to none. While they considered in vitro fertilization, they did not pursue it because of the small chance for success. Dave and Linda then decided to pursue adoption.

"We had to make a portfolio with lots of photos and with our biographies. I had a real problem with that. I thought whoever looked at our pictures would think Dave and I looked really old and then not want us to be the parents of their child. Age was a strike against me."

A few months later, Linda's sister mentioned that her daughter's friend had just had a baby girl. The girl was sixteen and was considering making an adoption plan for her baby, named Tori. Linda said she and Dave would like to be considered as parents.

A few months went by—nothing happened.

Then Linda received an unexpected and life-changing phone call. Another one of her sisters said the birth mother had decided she wanted Linda and Dave to adopt Tori—and she was bringing the baby to Linda. They had nothing for an infant, so while Linda waited, Dave made the first of many trips to buy diapers, formula, and other essentials.

"How naïve and innocent was that? You can't do that," Linda said, admitting you can't just take a woman's baby and give it to someone else. "Of course, this was not a fairy tale come true."

Within days the birth father told Dave and Linda he did not want his daughter to be adopted. Tori went back to her birth mom. Then, after having Tori for a visit, the birth father refused to bring Tori back to her birth mother.

Dave and Linda decided they wanted to help the birth mom. They hired a lawyer to protect her rights. A judge agreed that Tori must be returned to her birth mom.

Linda says, "I figured we would never get her back. Because the birth father was not paying any child support, we encouraged the lawyer to garnish his wages."

A month later, the birth father contacted Linda and said he agreed to Dave and Linda adopting Tori.

"The adoption process seemed like forever," Linda said. Both the birth mother and birth father had to be interviewed to ensure they were fit to make the decision to place Tori for adoption. Then came a ninety-day waiting period where either the birth mother or the birth father could change their minds. The birth parents could choose to waive the waiting period, allowing the adoption to become effective immediately.

"The birth dad told the adoption counselor he didn't have a problem signing the waiver, but I don't know if he signed it. The birth mom did not. We had to just wait while the birth mom thought about her decision. We were in limbo."

In the end, Linda and Dave adopted Tori when she was a year old. Linda says, "I would not want anyone else to go through what I went through. It was extremely painful. While we were waiting for the adoption to be final, my friends wanted to give me a baby shower. I wouldn't let them do it until that ninety-day period passed. I couldn't let myself have her as truly my own until then. I lived with the fear I would lose her.

"I love the fact that I am an older mom—and Tori loves me for who I am. I'll remind her that I am older than all her friends' moms and she'll say, 'I don't care, Mom.' I like that."

And, yes, Linda admitted it is embarrassing when people ask if she is Tori's grandmother. Tori, however, just ignores it and tells them that Linda is her mom.

"Older moms are better than younger moms," Linda said, while acknowledging she might be biased because of her experience. "We are better off financially. We have a better perspective on life that we can share with our child."

2

Advanced Maternal Age

Just Another Way of Saying I'm Old

> Your old ovaries give me hope.
>
> a thirtysomething,
> unmarried friend

Pregnancy is challenging enough without being inundated with statistics and tests underscoring the hazards of late-in-life motherhood. In addition to earning the AMA label, a woman is deluged with the risks of being an older pregnant woman: "Warning. Warning. Warning. There are potential complications for you—and for your unborn baby." What's a mommy-come-lately to do?

Out of Order

My life spun out of its expected orbit when I became pregnant.

At forty-one, I was most stressed by handing the car keys to my then seventeen-year-old son Josh and sitting in the passenger seat while he accelerated onto the highway. The reality of my pregnancy felt as if I had handed over the keys to my life—and I was barely hanging on.

My world shrank to the distance between my bed and the bathroom. I waged a losing battle with morning sickness compounded by emotional shock. I tried the age-old remedy of soda crackers and ginger ale. No relief. Suggested cures of sniffing fresh-cut lemons or eating beans or black olives failed. All-day nausea was a miserable way to manage my weight gain.

Sooner than I wanted, my clothes started feeling snug. I wondered if my body would ever rebound from the hormonal onslaught of this pregnancy. I told Rob that as an *old* pregnant woman at least I would have *new* maternity clothes. I felt lousy, but I'd look good. Yet the first time I reluctantly walked into a maternity shop, I couldn't bring myself to try on anything. Instead, I just wandered among the racks of elastic-paneled jeans and billowy tops.

"How are you today?" asked the way-too-chipper saleswoman.

"I guess I'm fine."

"Are you pregnant?"

"Yes—and I have a seventeen-year-old, a fourteen-year-old, and a twelve-year-old."

"That's nothing!" she said, "I once helped a woman who was eight months pregnant and the mother of the bride!"

Misery loves company.

Trendy maternity clothes notwithstanding, my AMA body struggled to adjust to all the changes. My first three pregnancies were uncomplicated. This time I experienced several episodes of mild bleeding.

The first time it happened, I delayed calling my doctor. Denial seemed easier than discovering something was wrong. When I finally called Dr. Campbell, he insisted I come in to be seen. But I resisted.

"I'm fine. I'm fine," I insisted.

"Yes, you are probably fine. But you need to come in to the hospital so I can examine you."

Despite my bravado, I was afraid. As I drove to the hospital, tears dripped down my face. I may not have planned this pregnancy, but I certainly didn't want to miscarry my baby.

Rob met me in Dr. Campbell's office. They escorted me to an ultrasound room. Nobody said anything. I dreaded what we would see—or not see—on the ultrasound. I was hooked up to a monitor and within seconds we heard my baby's steady heartbeat. It was an overwhelmingly comforting sound. After a thorough exam, Dr. Campbell announced that everything looked good but advised me to go on modified bed rest for a week. I stopped exercising, limiting my activity to sitting on the couch or lying in bed.

Thanksgiving and Christmas coincided with the last two months of my pregnancy. The day before Thanksgiving, close friends from out of town arrived for the long weekend. While Paul and Sara caught up on some sleep after driving all night, I worked on preparing the meal.

Throughout the morning, I felt a few sharp twinges in my back. As they increased in frequency, I called Rob to tell him I was having some odd pains. One minute I was talking to my husband. The next minute I was hanging onto the kitchen counter and throwing up in my sink.

I alternated between moaning and throwing up. Rob hung up, canceled his appointments, and rushed home. Paul and Sara staggered awake and calmed down the kids, who wondered what was wrong with me.

I wanted a shower but settled for awkwardly changing into clean clothes in the foyer. I couldn't possibly manage getting up the stairs to my bedroom. Then Rob and I took a wild ride to the birthing center. Paul and Sara went with us, while Josh and the girls followed in his car. I didn't want my uncontrolled screams to frighten my kids into never becoming parents.

The pain was agonizing. "I usually handle labor better than this," I told my friends between screams. Rob and Paul, who are family physicians, didn't think I was in labor. They were afraid my placenta was abrupting—tearing away from the uterus.

Pregnancy and Exercise

Dr. Mark Campbell says, "I tell my patients that if they were exercising before they got pregnant, they can continue exercising. If not, then I like to discuss choices with them."

Swimming, stationary cycling, walking, and low-impact aerobics are excellent workout choices for pregnant women. If you begin an exercise program after you become pregnant, check with your doctor about your workout. Here are some general tips:

Avoid exercising that causes pain, shortness of breath, or extreme tiredness.

Avoid activities like biking or skiing that increase your risk of falling.

Scuba diving is not recommended for pregnant women because of the danger of decompression sickness.

After the first trimester, avoid exercising while lying on your back because the weight of the baby may interfere with blood circulation.

Don't become overheated during your workout.

Stay well-hydrated.

Adjust your workout as your pregnancy progresses since changes in your weight may affect your balance and coordination.

If you live more than 6,000 feet above sea level, you may face added risks because of decreased oxygen. Avoid overexertion during exercise.

Until Dr. Campbell figured out what was wrong, I was denied any medication. In a haze of pain, I wondered if I could knock myself out by banging my head on the nearby counter. Sara took my hand and prayed for me and the baby. After too many hours of unmedicated torture, Rob and I spent the night while I "birthed" a kidney stone. Dr. Campbell prescribed morphine for me and then told the nurse, "Give her plenty. She's tall. She can handle it." That's when I knew I loved my doctor.

The next afternoon I arrived home, waved at our guests feasting on turkey and stuffing, and directed my exhausted body to bed. But first I called my brother Kenny who had experienced several kidney stones.

"It's true what they say: passing a kidney stone is worse than labor," I told him. "You have my deepest respect."

After this, labor and delivery would be a breeze.

Into the Unknown

Mary's late-in-life pregnancy thrust her into a world filled with unknowns. Despite being exhausted, she continued to work full-time. Her only other symptom of pregnancy was gagging every time she brushed her teeth. It seemed impossible to find "career" maternity clothes that didn't cost a fortune. Afraid she might miscarry, she decided to wait until the second trimester to tell anyone she was pregnant.

"The week we found out I was pregnant, we only told four people: my mom and my dad—who were thrilled; my best friend Sarah, whose daughter was pregnant at the same time; and our nephew."

They didn't want to tell anyone else until Mary was well past the risk of miscarriage.

"Around Valentine's Day, Doug told his mom I was pregnant. She didn't believe it. She said that some women think they are pregnant because they really want to be, but they aren't."

Unfortunately, Mary's first ob-gyn, who specialized in high-risk pregnancies, made a scary situation worse. He told her that 50 percent of women her age miscarry in the first trimester.

"During my second visit, the nurse called me an 'elderly mother'—despite the fact that I was in excellent shape. Then she told me that because of my age, my baby would test positive for every abnormality," Mary recalled. She cried for hours after hearing the "what could be wrong with the baby" list.

For three months Mary endured a landslide of negative information from the doctor and his nurse. When she was eighteen weeks pregnant, her doctor talked with her about having a triple screen test, a genetic screening blood test. Despite the fact that a triple screen is not a perfect test, he told her it would reveal all her baby's abnormalities. Even though the doctor said he could not make her have the test, Mary felt pressured.

"He gave me no encouragement—just grim statistics. I felt like I was battling his medical authority."

She sat in his office and sobbed. Without a word of reassurance, the doctor left while Mary and Doug decided what to do.

"Doug assured me everything would be okay. We finally gave in and decided to have the tests done. I did not want to know the results—ever. I was done hearing all the negative information."

Still crying, Mary told the doctor their decision. To this day her eyes fill with tears when she recalls his response: "If you wig out this weekend, call my office and they'll find someone to talk with you."

"I was a nonperson—and so was my baby. To him, my pregnancy was just statistics and data. But I was a human being, and he was not going to make me give up my baby. God gave me this baby, and I intended to keep him."

Mary left the office determined never to go back. When the receptionist said they needed to schedule a follow-up appointment, Mary said, "There will be no more appointments," and walked out. She spent two weeks researching her options for a new ob-gyn specializing in high-risk pregnancies.

Mary set up an interview with Dr. Dorine Day, who explained the risks of late-in-life pregnancy and why there were such concerns. She talked about what they could do medically and what they couldn't do. And she took the time to answer all Mary's questions about testing. Dr. Day also explained why she believed the tests were beneficial.

"Dr. Day was kind and understanding. She thought it was better to know if something was wrong with our baby before he was born. But she let Doug and me decide about testing. She was concerned about me and our baby and didn't overwhelm me with negative possibilities."

Mary focused on the positive during her pregnancy. Feeling her baby move reassured her—and his movements intensified as he grew.

With the concern of miscarriage diminishing each passing week and a supportive ob-gyn, Mary anticipated enjoying the rest of her pregnancy. A level two ultrasound—a comprehensive, total body evaluation also known as a targeted fetal scan—allayed her fears about common abnormalities. The ultrasound revealed she likely was having a boy—and that he was healthy. And at that point she had already told all her friends, family, and co-workers about her unexpected blessing.

"I was okay. The baby was okay. I knew things could still go wrong, but I was in good hands. I didn't suffer from morning sickness, but I did suffer intense fatigue. If I didn't eat enough protein in the morning to get jump-started, I was very weak. One morning I needed to go to another office to review proofs of an annual report. I was so weak I couldn't get out of my chair. I called Doug, who encouraged me to get some protein from the cafeteria. I did feel better after that—but when I got home from work I collapsed."

Since she didn't start showing until she was four and a half months along, Mary said it was easy to hide her pregnancy from her co-workers. Both Mary's boss and Doug's boss were shocked at their news—but were encouraging and happy for them too.

"I told the rest of my co-workers—twenty-five of them—by email. They all came rushing over to my office to congratulate me. They were so happy for me."

Then, during a routine appointment when Mary was eight months pregnant, Dr. Day discovered her amniotic fluid levels were low. Mary was restricted to complete bed rest.

"The goal was to allow time for the baby's lungs to develop. In one day I went from working full-time to sitting completely still on the couch and drinking ten glasses of water a day. I hadn't missed a day of work before then."

Four weeks later, Mary's amniotic fluid levels were continuing to drop. Dr. Day announced, "You're done. I can't allow this to go any further. You are going to the hospital immediately."

True Confession

I was a bit bossy with Dr. Campbell.

"You can write that I am of Advanced Maternal Age in my medical chart," I told him. "You can say it under your breath. But I do not want to *hear* you say it."

I was tired of being reminded that I was an old mom-to-be. My age felt like a gray cloud hanging over my pregnancy. I could not rewind my biological clock and be a young pregnant woman.

I was unaware of specific risks of an AMA pregnancy other than the increased likelihood of Down syndrome. And I didn't consider Down syndrome a "risk" so much as a possibility. Dr. Campbell kept me informed about different recommended medical tests, but he let Rob and me decide which ones to take.

Knowing that amniocentesis could cause a miscarriage, we decided not to have that test done. But we did want a level two ultrasound when I was about nineteen weeks along. Rob stood right behind the ultrasound technician and watched as our baby's body was illuminated in black and white on the monitor. We were thankful there were no indications of any physical problems—and surprised to be told we were having a third daughter. I was certain I was having a boy. So much for my maternal intuition!

> *Being a late-in-life mom is scary, but go for it! Children at any stage of life are the best and the worst thing that can happen to you. They steal your body, your freedom— you name it—but they return so much love and joy and delight.*
>
> Vikki, repeater mommy-come-lately at forty-two

The Bottom Line

If you got a wake-up call from your biological clock when you were thirty-five or even forty-five, so be it. Pick up the mantle of Advanced Maternal Age and wear it with pride!

Like me, you may have been surprised by an unexpected blessing. Or you may be like Mary, fighting against the onslaught of circumstances that delayed pregnancy or led you to adopt. Treasure your story. One day your child will ask about his or her beginnings, and you'll have the privilege of recounting it.

Cameo Appearance: **Karen**

Repeater mommy-come-lately at forty-one

Husband: **John**

Children: **Beth, age thirty; Emily, age fourteen**

According to Karen, she "turned the mental page past the baby possibility" when she turned forty. Then she found out she was pregnant when she was forty-one. Her daughter, Beth, was fifteen.

"I had a nasty virus that lingered on and on. It was only at a friend's insistence that I even had a pregnancy test."

When the test came back positive, Karen said, "I was in a major fog. I felt for a long time that if one day someone told me it was just a bad batch of pregnancy tests, I wouldn't have been a bit surprised."

One of the first people she told about her pregnancy was a friend who was also a midwife.

"Once the midwife stopped laughing, we got down to my biggest question: how much of a risk am I? She was honest but upbeat, always responding to my concerns with, 'That's not so bad.'"

Karen opted not to go through the full barrage of prenatal testing. She was having the baby—*no matter what the tests showed.*

"Why add risks and worries? I was well aware of possible age-related problems, and we decided to deal with whatever came once the baby was here."

During her pregnancy Karen developed gestational diabetes. Her midwife gave her a special diet and exercise regimen to follow. Karen promised to follow her instructions like they were written in stone, hoping to prevent any complications for herself or the baby.

"I felt great right after the birth and went home the next day. Being home made it much easier to connect with my newborn daughter."

Karen appreciated the good relationship she had with her maternity care provider. Because of her midwife's support, Karen was knowledgeable about the risks involved in her pregnancy—but chose not to worry about them.

Cameo Appearance: **Lisa**

Repeater mommy-come-lately at thirty-eight, thirty-nine, and forty-two

Husband: **Clark**

Children: **Jeffrey, age nineteen; Jared, age seventeen; Joanna, age fourteen; Janelle, age twelve; Jacob, age seven; Jonathan, age six; Jennifer, age three**

Lisa was thirty-nine when her sixth child, Jonathan, was born.

The possibility of Down syndrome was raised during her pregnancy when an ultrasound showed a fluid-filled cyst on the baby's neck. Although the cyst eventually resolved, it still "marked" him as having a higher risk of having a chromosomal abnormality.

"I chose not to have amniocentesis. I'd miscarried previously and was not willing to take the risk of the procedure causing a miscarriage. I had numerous doctor visits and ultrasounds. They found at least one other marker that could indicate a problem and said the baby had a one-in-fifty chance of having some chromosomal abnormality."

Lisa and her husband chose not to worry about the possibility of problems—deciding instead to trust God to give them the baby who was right for their family.

"When Jonathan was born and we discovered he did have Down syndrome, we never saw it as a tragedy. We rejoiced that he was alive and here with us. My biggest fear was that he would have a problem that would not allow him to survive, so Down syndrome seemed like no big deal."

In spite of Jonathan having difficulty feeding and gaining weight, Lisa said she went through Jonathan's first year feeling like she was "the most blessed, luckiest woman in the world. Of course, I felt blessed when I had all my children, but this was stronger—a very strong, almost physical feeling."

Three years later Lisa had her seventh child at age forty-two.

"Before that daughter was born, I looked forward to having that strong feeling of blessing again. I thought I would feel it even stronger, especially since she was normal and healthy," Lisa said.

But the intense feeling never came.

Lisa said, "It was then I realized that God gave me that feeling as a special gift to help me deal with the difficulties of Jonathan's first year."

3

Just the Facts, Mom

I feel like every time I walked into my doctor's office, my
medical chart set off alarms: Old lady! Old lady!

Jane, repeater mommy-come-lately at forty-four

Why the "magic thirty-five"? Why does turning thirty-five
earn a pregnant woman the title of Advanced Maternal
Age (AMA)?

Research supports the belief that risks—both to mom and
baby—increase as women get older. While it may make us
feel old, the AMA label does put doctors on the lookout for
problems and encourages a greater level of caution during
pregnancy.

Down syndrome is one possible condition doctors want to test
for in the case of an AMA pregnancy. When a woman is thirty-five
years old at her estimated date of delivery, her chance of having
a baby with Down syndrome is equal to her chance of having a
miscarriage associated with second trimester amniocentesis.

Because some medical providers assume a woman would abort a baby with Down syndrome, the possibility of miscarriage is deemed an acceptable risk of amniocentesis. However, Dr. Campbell notes that "the miscarriage rate due to amniocentesis is lower now than it was ten years ago. If you are in the hands of a good maternal fetal medical specialist—another title for an ob-gyn subspecialist—an amniocentesis is not so risky." In early 2007, The American College of Obstetricians and Gynecologists (ACOG) recommended that amniocentesis be offered to all pregnant patients, regardless of age.

Most AMA pregnancies turn out very well, according to Dr. Campbell, who acknowledged that sometimes maternity care providers suggest invasive diagnostic tests such as amniocentesis or chorionic villus sampling (CVS) too often. He says, "When I talk to my patients, I stress the importance of a level two ultrasound. If nothing shows up on the ultrasound, I offer the amniocentesis, but I emphasize the normal ultrasound. I always let the patient make the decision—but it is an informed decision."

Managing the Avalanche

Medical information about increased risks for both a mommy-come-lately and her baby can hit a woman like an avalanche. How can you wade through the warnings so you aren't overwhelmed by worry throughout your pregnancy?

Although maternity care providers may stress prenatal testing, remember that most pregnancies turn out very well. As I talked with my doctor, my physician husband, and other late-in-life moms, the overall opinion was to accent the positive while recognizing—but not overemphasizing—the negative. Be informed, be prepared, and then, as is true in any pregnancy, choose not to worry.

Straight Talk about Medical Risks for Mommies-Come-Lately

Having a baby is somewhat risky business at any age—but risks increase when a woman is thirty-five years or older. Concerns include increased risk of:

Infertility

Women ages thirty-five to thirty-nine have a 22 percent risk of infertility.

Women ages forty to forty-four have a 28.7 percent risk of infertility.

Miscarriage

Women age thirty-five have a 20 percent risk of miscarriage.

Women age forty have a 34 percent risk of miscarriage.

Women age forty-five have a 53 percent risk of miscarriage.

Chromosomal abnormalities such as Down syndrome

For a twenty-year-old woman, the risk of having a baby with Down syndrome is 1 in 1,400.

For a thirty-year-old, it is 1 in 900.

For a thirty-five-year-old, it is 1 in 290.

For a forty-year-old, it is 1 in 100.

Other complications

AMA women may develop high blood pressure or diabetes for the first time during pregnancy.

They may develop preeclampsia, a complication involving elevated blood pressure and kidney problems.

Preterm delivery and low birth weight babies are more common.

What's Up with Weeks, Months, and Trimesters?

Medical practitioners may use different terms to describe the age of an unborn baby. Health professionals calculate by weeks because it is a more accurate measure of fetal growth and development. Typically, the gestational age is calculated from the last menstrual period to define the age of the baby. This is an accepted convention in spite of the fact that a woman cannot become pregnant until ovulation—normally two weeks after her last period. A woman's estimated date of delivery is forty weeks from the first day of her last menstrual period. For those of you who are detail oriented, a normal pregnancy is about 280 days. I'd rather not think about pregnancy in terms of hundreds of days!

In lay terms, pregnancy lasts nine months. Trimesters roughly divide the forty-week pregnancy into thirds. The first trimester ends between thirteen and fourteen weeks. The second trimester ends between twenty-seven and twenty-eight weeks. And of course the third trimester ends when your baby is born—usually between thirty-seven and forty-two weeks.

Be Healthy, Stay Healthy

If pregnancy is postponed until your midthirties or later, it is advantageous to take care of yourself. Here are the basic things you need to do to maintain your health:

1. Maintain a healthy weight and body mass index (BMI). BMI is the measure of body fat based on height and weight. Being overweight can exacerbate medical conditions like diabetes or high blood pressure. You can find a BMI calculator at http://nhlbisupport.com/bmi/.
2. Exercise. Being in good physical condition benefits you during your pregnancy as well as during labor and delivery.
3. Take folic acid. Nutritional guidelines now recommend that *any woman of childbearing age* take a multivitamin with 400 micrograms of folic acid to help prevent neural tube defects. The neural tube is the precursor of the central nervous system that includes the brain and spinal cord. Because the neural tube closes within weeks of conception, a woman should definitely be taking folic acid one month prior to getting pregnant. Folic acid has to be well

established on a cellular level to ensure that the tube closes correctly.

4. Don't smoke. If you do smoke cigarettes, stop—preferably before you get pregnant.

5. Don't drink alcohol if you are trying to get pregnant or during your pregnancy.

6. Do Kegel exercises. Such exercises involve repeatedly tightening and releasing the pelvic muscle. They help maintain the strength and tone of your pelvic floor muscles.

7. Check your immunizations prior to conception. Ensure you are immune to rubella and chicken pox (varicella). If not, be immunized for both chicken pox and rubella at least three months before getting pregnant.

8. Have your thyroid checked prior to pregnancy. If you are hypothyroid—when your thyroid is not functioning well—it is usually easily treatable. Proper thyroid levels will help prevent maternal and fetal complications during pregnancy.

Take care of your emotional health too. Maintain relationships that offer you encouragement and support. Take time to do things that you enjoy, whether that is reading or hiking or sewing.

Don't Ignore Your Teeth

Dentists recommend that pregnant women who have good dental health have their teeth cleaned every three months rather than every six months. Dentist Dr. Stephen Calendine says, "If the mother-to-be has been diagnosed with gum disease or periodontal disease, we may sometimes recommend checkups every one to two months."

He explained that pregnancy hormones can ravage oral tissues and added that pregnancy gingivitis (inflamed gums due to bacterial plaque building up on teeth) is a frequent occurrence—even if a woman had good oral health before she became pregnant.

"Periodontal disease, which is advanced gum disease involving loss of bone and teeth and gum abscesses, is an autoimmune disease that sometimes lies dormant until a person experiences significant emotional or physical stress, such as pregnancy," Dr. Calendine said. "We now know that premature labor and other potentially debilitating complications can be directly related to untreated periodontal disease."

Emotional Upheaval

Pregnancy can also bring about emotional struggles ranging from mild to severe.

"The blues" is a normal phenomenon that occurs in 70 percent of postpartum patients, according to Dr. Campbell. "Symptoms—including weeping, restlessness, headache, irritability, and insomnia—occur within the first week to ten days after a woman gives birth and usually resolve quickly. It is not normal when 'the blues' last longer than ten to fourteen days. When 'the blues' becomes extended, a woman is dealing with postpartum depression.

"Eight to 20 percent of women experience postpartum depression. That's one in five, so it is still pretty common." He also notes, "A woman can experience postpartum depression up to a year after giving birth. It's important to remember that this is treatable. Don't give up hope."

Most medical practitioners administer a questionnaire to screen for postpartum depression. (See the Postpartum Depression Quiz on p. 187.)

Postpartum psychosis is much worse than postpartum depression and occurs in 0.1 percent of women. It usually occurs in women who have some past personal history or family history of psychosis.

"Postpartum psychosis can occur two to three days postpartum — or even several months later," according to Dr. Campbell. "A woman experiences schizophrenia or paranoia and an increased level of anxiety and suicidal thoughts."

If you are experiencing emotional struggles, please talk to your doctor — your emotional health is just as important for you and your baby as your physical health.

Pick Your Maternity Care Provider Wisely

No mommy-come-lately wants to be continually bombarded with everything that could go wrong with her pregnancy. Nor does she want to be called elderly. Excuse me? Even my eighty-eight-year-old mother-in-law does not want to be called elderly!

Decide if you are going to see an ob-gyn, a family practice physician, or a midwife for your prenatal care and delivery. The list below defines the training of these different medical practitioners.

Family physician: This is a doctor who specializes in a full spectrum of family medicine, which can include maternity care. After graduating from medical school, a family physician completes a three-year residency program focusing on integrated care for all ages. Depending on their training, some family physicians may perform C-sections.

Obstetrician-gynecologist (ob-gyn): This specialist focuses on women's health, primarily related to reproductive organ systems. Ob-gyns receive four years of surgical and medical training after medical school.

Perinatologist (also called a high-risk obstetrician or a maternal fetal medicine specialist): This is an ob-gyn who completes an additional three-year fellowship after residency in order to specialize in high-risk pregnancies.

Midwives: The majority of midwives are either Certified Nurse-Midwives (CNM) or Certified Midwives (CM). CNMs are licensed healthcare professionals who are educated in both nursing and midwifery. They provide primary health care to pregnant women, including prenatal and labor and delivery care. A CM is educated solely in midwifery and provides care similar to a CNM. Midwife-assisted births can occur either at home or at a hospital.

In addition to a medical practitioner, you may also include a *doula* in your support system. A doula is usually a woman who has experienced childbirth. She is trained to provide physical and emotional support to women during labor and delivery. Doulas do not perform clinical tasks; their role is to provide continual emotional reassurance and comfort.

If you're planning to get pregnant—no matter what your age—it is common practice to set up a preconception counseling appointment with your maternity care provider. This allows you a chance to discuss your plans and health concerns with a medical professional before you get pregnant. Keep researching your options and interviewing providers until you find the right medical provider for you.

A word of caution: *do not delay getting medical care.* If you are more than twenty weeks pregnant when you seek prenatal care, some physicians may not accept you as a patient because of medical/legal concerns. Sometimes their malpractice insurers restrict them from seeing patients who are "late entrants to care." Connect with a physician or midwife early in your pregnancy for healthcare reasons as well.

Control Preexisting Conditions

High blood pressure, diabetes, asthma, or thyroid disorders should be under control if possible before getting pregnant. Ideally, you want to manage these conditions with medications you can continue to use during pregnancy without posing a risk to your baby. However, once you are pregnant, you may need to change medications. Either way, your physician will monitor you more closely.

> *I was approached more than once to consider abortion — mainly because my initial response to this pregnancy wasn't real positive. I was reminded of cutoff dates of certain "procedures." This shocked me more than my pregnancy. I couldn't understand why it was even mentioned to a married, healthy woman.*
>
> Janet, repeater mommy-come-lately at thirty-five

Here is a description of the most common prenatal tests.

First Trimester

Ultrasound—An ultrasound machine uses sound waves that reflect off the baby to create a computer-generated image. Often a first-trimester ultrasound is more accurate in determining gestational age—how old the baby is—than using the dates of a woman's last menstrual period.

An example of an abnormal finding from a first-trimester ultrasound is a nuchal translucency. This is an increased skin fold thickness in the neck of the fetus; it can be determined between the eleventh and thirteenth week of pregnancy. The thickened skin fold is most likely because of delayed development of the lymphatic system. First-trimester screening using nuchal translucency and two blood tests—pregnancy-associated plasma protein-A and free beta-HCG—have comparable detection rates and positive screening rates for Down syndrome as the quad screening test (see below) done in the second trimester.

Chorionic villus sampling (CVS)—CVS is a first-trimester invasive test that involves sampling tissue between the placenta and uterus. A thin plastic tube is normally inserted through the cervix and guided to the placenta, where cells are extracted. It is performed between ten and twelve weeks. The advantage of CVS over amniocentesis is that the results are available earlier in the pregnancy. Medical practitioners are able to get the information needed about genetic abnormalities 99 percent of the time. CVS has a 1 to 1.5 percent miscarriage rate.

Second Trimester

Ultrasound—A second-trimester ultrasound is an excellent tool to examine the anatomy of the baby. Abnormalities such as heart or brain defects can often be identified during this stage of pregnancy.

Strive for a team approach between you and your nutritionist, nurse, primary care physician, and maternity care provider. Expect to have extra appointments and blood draws and possibly twenty-four-hour urine tests.

Amniocentesis—This is an invasive screening test. The procedure involves inserting a needle through the mother's abdomen into the uterus to collect a sample of the amniotic fluid surrounding the baby. This test is performed between fifteen and twenty weeks. It has a miscarriage rate of 0.5 percent and a 1 to 2 percent rate of complications such as vaginal bleeding or leakage of amniotic fluid. Early amniocentesis can be performed from eleven to thirteen weeks; however, it has a higher miscarriage and complication rate than traditional amniocentesis.

Quad screen—This is a maternal blood test usually done between fifteen to twenty weeks. The best time to obtain this test is between sixteen to eighteen weeks. The quad screen tests for four things:

1. *Maternal serum alpha-fetoprotein* is proteins made by the baby found in the mother's blood. Levels either too high or too low can be suggestive of neural tube defects such as spina bifida or chromosomal abnormalities like Down syndrome. Other conditions are also associated with high or low levels, such as twins or triplets or vaginal bleeding.

2. *Human chorionic gonadotropin (HCG)* is a hormone produced by a woman's placenta during pregnancy.

3. *Estriol* is also a hormone made by the mother.

4. *Inhibin A* is a glycoprotein. Levels are elevated in women carrying a baby with Down syndrome.

The values of all four tests from a single blood specimen are used to more accurately predict risk of neural tube defects or chromosomal abnormalities. Blood values vary depending on the age of the fetus. Therefore, accurate gestational age is important to ensure that the risk prediction is valid. If a quad screen returns abnormal, an ultrasound may be performed to ensure accurate gestational age.

Be Informed about Genetic Counseling and Testing

As an AMA mom-to-be, you will probably be offered counseling because of your increased risk for genetic defects such as Down syndrome. Listen to the professional advice, and then make your decisions based on your personal values. Some women choose to have tests done so they can emotionally prepare if their baby has a genetic disorder. In rare instances, screening tests may help diagnose correctable nongenetic problems.

The Bottom Line

Once you are labeled AMA, be prepared for an onslaught of medical options. Be knowledgeable about the medical tests that will be recommended to you. Understand the benefits and risks of each test. Talk with your medical provider about your options—and then make your decisions.

For additional information, check out the links to medical websites listed in the Resources section of my website www .MommyComeLately.com.

If you plan to wait until you are older to have children, look over the "Be Healthy, Stay Healthy" segment in this chapter and develop a plan to maintain your health.

≡ Cameo Appearance: **Roxanne**

Repeater mommy-come-lately at age thirty-five, thirty-seven, forty-two (stillborn son), and forty-five

Husband: **Jack**

Children: **Daniel, age twenty; Stephen, age eighteen; Kara and Suzanne, twins, age seventeen; Josh, age ten; Jamie, age eight; Peter, age one**

Despite having four children, Roxanne wanted another baby.

"My friends and family thought I was crazy, and none of them were shy about telling me so. In my twenties, I had three pregnancies—including twins—in three years,"

Roxanne said. "My twin daughters were five; my sons were six-and-a-half and eight years old. But I longed for a baby."

So she and her husband Jack talked and prayed about it. They decided to have Jack's vasectomy reversed and started trying for their "second family."

"We thought we were finished having babies, so I had to replace everything. I missed my favorite maternity clothes," Roxanne said. "The styles were not created with an older mom in mind. I didn't want to wear skintight maternity clothing and show the world my middle-aged Buddha shape."

Within a few years, they added two more children to their family. Her son Joshua was born when she was thirty-five, and her son Jamie was born when she was thirty-seven.

Several years later, at age forty-two, Roxanne once again stared at the tiny pink lines of a positive pregnancy test.

"This time I had made plans that didn't include a pregnancy. I had four sons, ages sixteen, fourteen, six, and four. I also had twin thirteen-year-old daughters," she said. "I tried to remain calm by repeating my mantra 'Children are a blessing.' I didn't see how I could cope with one more thing on my plate—especially since we had completed a cross-country move two days before I found out I was pregnant."

Her late-in-life pregnancies were tougher than her twentysomething pregnancies. Because Roxanne was homeschooling, she had little time to slow down for morning sickness. Roxanne suffered through four months of nausea while working through the emotions of an unplanned pregnancy—shock, resentment, unhappiness, and finally acceptance.

"I realized God wasn't calling only me to have this baby. He was giving my family a new child. I reached beyond acceptance and embraced the pregnancy. I made room in my heart and room in my life for a new baby."

Then—heartbreak.

At nineteen weeks, during a routine office visit, Roxanne learned that her baby did not have a heartbeat. She delivered her stillborn son Zachary a week later.

"It didn't make any sense," Roxanne said. "But I know God had his own reason for placing Zachary Joseph Sherwood into my womb and into my family for a short time—even though we couldn't keep him. Now the thought of heaven is a bit sweeter to me because someday I'll get to meet Zachary."

Devastated, Roxanne wanted to get pregnant immediately, although her husband wanted to wait a few months while she recovered physically. As months passed, she became fearful of the possibility of birth defects because of her age. Her arms felt empty, and she imagined what life would be like if Zachary had lived. Each month the arrival of her menstrual period started an emotional roller coaster.

"I bounced from 'I hope I am' to 'I'm relieved I'm not.' Although I longed for the opportunity to raise Zachary, after eighteen months I told God that I was content with my family."

Six months later, Roxanne discovered she was pregnant again. She says, "This time, I didn't spend one minute worrying about how old I was or wondering how this baby would change our plans. I wanted my baby to feel loved every minute I carried him."

The pregnancy was difficult, with morning sickness lasting more than four months.

"I had about a month of feeling okay, but that month was December. I had to do all the Christmas shopping and catch up on so many things I'd let slide," Roxanne said. "Then I started having heartburn and my hips ached. It was painful to get out of a chair or out of bed. I couldn't stand for any length of time. By my seventh month, I shopped from a wheelchair."

Roxanne was also moodier than with her previous pregnancies.

"Some of my emotional swings were affected by dealing with four teenagers. When I was tired—which was almost all the time—it really irked me if my teens didn't do their chores. I also worried about miscarrying again. While I didn't like the Advanced Maternal Age label, I felt every one of my forty-five years."

At times Roxanne felt embarrassed. "When I was seven months pregnant, I attended a college honor society induction for my son and looked clearly out of place," she said. At eight months pregnant, Roxanne and her husband Jack celebrated their twenty-first wedding anniversary by giving one another what they needed most: baby furniture.

Supported by her husband and two teenage daughters, Roxanne gave birth to a healthy son, whom they named Peter. "He's wonderful. I fell in love with him right away. My mom began menopause at forty-three, so I never imagined having another baby at my age. But I'm so glad God blessed us with Peter," she said.

Roxanne said Jack talks about retiring when he is sixty-seven—when Peter graduates from college at age twenty-two. "The thought is even more incredible when we realize our other children will be twenty-nine, thirty-one, thirty-eight, thirty-nine, and forty-one," she said.

4

Everything Is Back to Normal— Except Me

I put on my best happy face and smiled when they told me the good news. Inside I was so conflicted. Did I want to be pregnant? I didn't think so. Then I felt guilt. What loving mom wouldn't want to be blessed with another child? How am I supposed to feel? I was kind of hoping I was on my way to more "me" time with older kids.

Susie, repeater mommy-come-lately at thirty-eight, with thirteen- and eleven-year-old sons and an almost two-year-old daughter

Ah, childbirth. That word sounds so much nicer than *labor*. Women love to talk about childbirth. Giving birth is a female rite of passage. Telling our labor and delivery stories is a hard-earned privilege that creates a special bond between women. Think about it: have you ever heard *dads* swapping birthing stories? Usually men leave the room when their wives start talking about things like amniotic fluid, back labor, and transition. We talk about our doctors, our coaches, how many hours (down to the second!) we labored, and how we pushed until we felt like our faces would explode—and then had a cesarean section.

My first three deliveries were quick and drug-free, and I planned on the same for my fourth. But this time around, labor and delivery proved more complicated.

Well into my ninth month, I woke up in the middle of the night knowing something was happening. Had my water broken? When I tried to wake Rob up, he grumbled a skeptical "Probably not" and rolled over to go back to sleep. I wanted

Oh, the Things People Say!

Years before a woman even thinks about having children, she may face the question "Why aren't you pregnant yet?" And once she becomes pregnant, the invasion of her privacy continues. Pregnancy turns a woman into some sort of walking, talking piece of public property. Without even asking "Would you mind?" strangers touch your tummy and then ask questions like:

When are you due?
Is it a boy or a girl?
Are you having any more children?
Are you going to breastfeed?

When Alice started having her children in her mid-to-late thirties, people told her, "It's about time!"

When Rob and I told people I was pregnant, someone said, "I thought Rob was fixed." I didn't know whether to explain that you "fix" a dog or inform her that our "reproductive choices" were personal and private. I just ignored the comment.

One person asked me if my caboose kid had the same father as my first three children. Others asked me if I was going to have any more children—even as I reeled from the shock of this pregnancy.

"You need to have another child so Christa has a sibling," someone said.

"Christa does have siblings—three of them," I pointed out. "They are just a lot older than she is."

Early in her pregnancy, when Susie struggled to be happy about having a baby at thirty-eight, someone told her, "Well, at least it isn't cancer."

to shout, "Told you so!" when the nurse at the birthing center said to come in.

When I went into labor with Amy, our third child, we dropped Josh and Katie Beth off with friends. This fourth time we woke up all three kids and waited while they got dressed. Just as they did during the kidney stone adventure, they followed us to the birthing center. Unlike our escapade a few weeks before, I was calm, cool, and collected.

I could do this.

The center was quiet at 2:00 a.m. Rob and the girls followed me into the birthing room while Josh opted to leaf through outdated hunting magazines in the waiting area. Dr. Campbell arrived and prayed with all of us. Then we got down to the business of my having a baby.

Nothing happened.

Despite strong contractions, my cervix refused to dilate. *Was it just too old and tired?*

Rob and I walked slow laps around the nurses' desk, hoping to jump-start my labor. Josh napped on the couch in the birthing room while the girls sat around looking bored. The nurses offered them Christmas cookies and encouraged me to deliver before their shift ended. A friend came and took the kids out for breakfast while Rob and I discussed options with Dr. Campbell.

Eight discouraging hours after my water broke, I agreed to an epidural and pitocin. A nurse sat beside my bed watching every blip, bleep, and bloop on multiple monitors attached to me and the baby.

Less than thirty minutes later, I complained to Rob about being nauseated. The nurse examined me and, with a look of surprise, announced I was completely dilated. As she went to get Dr. Campbell, Rob said, "You know, I could deliver this baby, but let's wait for Mark to get here."

Amy videotaped Katie Beth's wide-eyed amazement as she watched Christa being born. Katie Beth helped her dad coach my breathing. She also cut the umbilical cord. Josh opted not to be there for the delivery—which was fine with me. Instead he waited outside, performing card tricks for the nurses. He met Christa when she was just a few minutes old.

With "Silent Night" playing in the background, Christa Jean Vogt was born on Christmas Eve of the year 2000 at 11:39 a.m. Watching Rob hold our new daughter was a surreal moment. Yes, I'd just gone through labor and delivery. But there was still a part of me that couldn't believe I had a newborn daughter.

Unto Us a Child Is Born

Josh was responsible for sending the "She's here!" email after Christa was born. The subject line read *"Unto us a child is born"* — and then he wrote:

Specifically, a little girl named Christa Jean Vogt.

No surprise baby boy. Born yesterday on Christmas Eve, December 24th, at 11:39 a.m., Christa weighed 8 pounds 4 ounces, and was 20 inches long. We in the Vogt household are very thankful for a safe delivery both for the mother and baby. After being checked out by the doctors, she was proclaimed "perfect." The mother is doing very well, being just a bit tired but getting some good rest. They recently returned home from the hospital, and we are introducing Christa to the house. Thank you all for your prayers.

It is an interesting concept, realizing that our family will never be the same again. We are now six instead of five. We have three girls instead of two. I am the older brother of three now. Christa is going to have to go through all of school, even as the three of us will have graduated by the time she enters kindergarten. She is someone who we know nothing about at this point. God has given her to us (without our even asking) and now we will do our best to raise her as He would desire, loving her and helping her grow up in this world.

Hopefully, you all will get to see her at some time or the other. She is quite cute. At this point the girls are saying she looks like my father, but only time will tell. She has dark hair and blue eyes, but that may change over time.

Thanks for all the love, prayers, and help you have given over this pregnancy.

Love to all,

Josh for the Vogts

Emotions: 'Round and 'Round and 'Round They Go, and Where They'll Stop, Nobody Knows!

Both my grandmothers and one great-grandmother had caboose babies. My pregnancy at thirty-eight was like part of an unplanned family tradition. That made it easier on me. However, I was depressed because we were trying to sell our house and move to Florida where my husband had already been transferred by the Coast Guard.

Karen, mommy-come-lately at thirty-nine

We were absolutely stunned! How did this happen?

Susie, mommy-come-lately at thirty-eight

My husband and I accomplished every goal we had set before we had a baby. I supported my husband as he established a successful career. I had my dream job. We bought the perfect family home. I was elated when our ultimate goal—pregnancy—was achieved.

Scoti, mommy-come-lately at thirty-five

My reaction to being pregnant was a mixture of total shock, disbelief, and absolute joy.

Mary, mommy-come-lately at forty-six

I was definitely stunned. After a number of years of debate with my husband and even trying to get pregnant, we had made plans for the future—just the two of us.

Janet, mommy-come-lately at thirty-five

My heart is to look a miracle from God in the face—to realize this baby is my gift, my miracle.

Jane, mommy-come-lately at forty-four

Reeling from Reality

I had a life—and it was going forward.

Christa's arrival slammed me into reverse.

Rob and I were preparing to launch Josh out of the nest and off to college. I was beginning to let go of my firstborn, and I found my arms filled with a baby. Christa's needs gave me no time to process my emotions about Josh leaving home. Overwhelmed, I just stuffed my feelings and planned on dealing with them later.

Within a few weeks of Christa's birth, Rob's job situation imploded. He came home one night and told me about the trouble at work. Sitting on the bedroom floor with Christa in my arms, I responded, "I'm sorry. I can't help you through this. I don't know what to do. I am physically, mentally, and emotionally exhausted."

So much for supporting my husband.

There was just too much to handle. Christa was just one more thing. *One more unplanned, major thing.*

All three kids promised to help with Christa. Rob and I were amazed at how they had stepped up to the plate during my pregnancy. But I knew who was going to take care of this baby: *me.*

When Christa was born, the kids were on Christmas break. We had a couple weeks of "All for one and one for all." And then Josh and the girls returned to school. Rob's time off ended, and he walked back into a volatile work situation. I resented their getting back to their lives when I had lost mine.

Resentment. Now that is not a traditional family value.

Most of my tears were shed in the privacy of my bedroom, dripping into my journal or onto my baby's face. I loved my family, but I was angry with them.

"Everyone gets to go back to normal," I told Rob. "Everybody but me!"

More of the Same

If Mary's first ob-gyn was "the doctor from hell," her labor and delivery lived up to the label too.

When her amniotic fluid levels continued to drop, Dr. Day decided to induce her.

"I didn't even get to go home and pack a bag for the hospital," Mary said.

Mary was induced at 2:00 p.m., and the first six hours of labor were uneventful. While Mary progressed slowly, Doug took a few naps. About 2:00 a.m. the next day, the nurses suggested an epidural. During the procedure, Doug heard the anesthesiologist mumble, "Uh-oh." The needle had hit spinal fluid. When the doctor came back to check on her thirty minutes later, he discovered Mary was numb from her neck down.

The doctor stopped the procedure to allow the medication to dissipate. After several more hours, they restarted the epidural. Five hours later, Mary knew things were starting to happen. Another three hours later, Mary repeatedly insisted she was "an old horse" and demanded that they "get the baby out."

Forty-five minutes later, Justin Neal Darr was born, at 10:05 a.m. on August 1, 2001. But after enduring twenty hours of labor, Mary wasn't able to enjoy her long-awaited child. Instead, her doctor spent the next hour repairing a third-degree perineal tear—one requiring a total of one hundred stitches.

Doug and the nurses helped take care of Justin during the five days Mary stayed in the hospital. Suffering from painful spinal headaches, she had to lie flat most of the time.

And Now for Something Completely Different

Before becoming a mommy-come-lately, Mary worked for twenty-six years. She loved her communications job, earned a good income, and was progressing up the corporate ladder.

Both Mary's and Doug's careers changed after Justin was born. Mary had three months of family leave that started when she was put on bed rest. A few weeks before Justin's birth, Doug was promoted and then asked to consider running for sheriff. Before then Doug had planned on adjusting his schedule so he could take care of Justin while Mary worked. When Doug decided to run for sheriff, Mary asked her boss if she could work part-time, twenty hours a week.

"I could find child care for twenty hours each week," she says. "My employer tried to make my new schedule work out, but it just didn't. My boss was very disappointed. But I chose to stay home because it was the best decision for me, for Justin, and for our family. Our lives had already been turned upside down by a late-

> *When I first started this mom journey, I was looking for someone to tell me what was normal as a late-in-life mom. What I find most different is that, for late-in-life moms, so much of our lives are already established. We have longstanding careers and activities and things that are important that comprise our lives. So the question is, How do you fit the new life of "Mommy" in with the already established life?*
>
> Marlo, repeater mommy-come-lately at thirty-five and again at almost thirty-eight

in-life baby. Now we were heading into a strenuous political campaign. Doug made 275 appearances during his successful campaign for sheriff—and we moved into another house too."

At forty-six, Mary became a first-time stay-at-home mother.

"I knew I made the right decision. That was never in question. That doesn't change the fact that I cried my eyes out for six weeks. It was hard to say good-bye to everything familiar. When I let go of my dream job, the grief was so intense. The transition was so, so difficult. I missed talking to my co-workers on a daily basis. I didn't know any other mothers with babies. Most of my friends were already *grandparents* of preschoolers. Yes, I was taking care of my baby and loving every minute of it. But at the same time, I felt so isolated and alone."

Got a Life

So what's the big deal? What's the difference between a mommy-come-lately and a twentysomething mom?

The most significant difference is time. With extra years—even decades—behind them, most women in their thirties and forties have established some kind of life. Maybe not the life of their dreams—but then again, maybe it is. Late-in-life motherhood happens in the midst of a variety of life situations:

A woman catches the first glimpse of an empty nest and new possibilities for her life—and she discovers she's pregnant.

A woman delays having children while she achieves career or ministry goals.

The long-awaited "Mr. Right" arrives, albeit a few years later than originally planned.

A couple grieves when infertility strangles their desire to start a family.

Divorce ends the "I do's" and dashes any hopes for children.

Women and men remarry and become parents of a blended family.

Whatever your situation, you probably had come to terms with it—maybe even poured everything you had into it—before late-in-life motherhood intervened. Now everything you thought you knew seems turned upside down. As Jane Jarrell, author of the book *Secrets of a Midlife Mom*, put it: "A woman having children when she is thirty or forty clashes with what she has been pursuing her whole life. It rocks her world."

Mary and I represent two types of late-in-life moms: the "There must be some mistake, because I don't want to be pregnant" woman and the "I've waited and prayed and pursued this day" woman.

Whether you are a forty-one-year-old first-time mom or have a "caboose baby" like I do, being a mommy-come-lately alters the flow of your life. Life as you know it becomes life as you knew it. Relationships change—with your spouse, with your other children, with your extended family, and with your friends.

Crying until I Laughed

Susie was my first close friend to join me as a mommy-come-lately. She said her unexpected pregnancy at thirty-eight felt like she was trying to swallow a shag carpet. She felt guilty because she didn't want her life to be interrupted by a newborn.

"Whatever you are feeling is valid," I assured her.

I wish someone had told me that.

I didn't laugh for the first few months of my pregnancy. At the beginning of my second trimester, Katie Beth and Amy persuaded me to go into a baby clothing store. Within seconds they were showing me one cute outfit after another. On one shelf I found a tiny yellow layette gown covered with roly-poly hamsters. Something about their whimsical frolicking across the fabric tickled me. I bought the matching cap and gown just because it made me laugh.

Finding humor in an infant outfit was my first step toward embracing my life as a mommy-come-lately. Laughter diffused the tension caused by my ambivalent emotions. I needed time to untangle the knots of dismay and fear. Yes, part of me eagerly anticipated holding my child. After all, I like my first three children. Why wouldn't I like my fourth?

I also clung to the assurances from other women that Christa would be a special blessing to our family. Tucked away in Christa's baby book are notes I received during my pregnancy. Each and every one said the same thing: my life

Simply Stated

With thanks to my friend Janet, here is one mommy-come-lately's quick take on the advantages and disadvantages of having a caboose kid.

Benefits:

Seeing life from a child's point of view again

Making sure family vacations happen with fun side trips

Rediscovering playgrounds and fast-food restaurants with play areas

Acquiring lots of fresh anecdotes for writing projects

Challenges:

Getting used to noise and a messy house again

Struggling with energy and strength issues

Dealing with being mistaken for the grandma

would be profoundly changed—for the better—by Christa's arrival.

"Whoever this precious gift may be," wrote one friend, "I know you will soon be able to treasure each moment."

"Okay, God," I wrote in my journal, "I'm trusting that your plan for our family is to bless us with Christa."

What's a Mommy-Come-Lately to Do?

Becoming a late-in-life mom sent my emotions on an out-of-control roller-coaster ride. If I had to do it over again, I'd sit back, fasten my seat belt, and hold on. The ride is worth all the ups and downs. What about you? How can you navigate your mixed feelings about being an older mom?

Know that your ambivalent feelings are normal and that being thrilled, scared, happy, and sad all at the same time is allowed.

Even if having a baby is a dream come true for you, realize embracing one dream (motherhood) might mean letting go of another dream (career or ministry).

Be gentle with yourself while you adjust to being a mommy-come-lately. Whether the blues hit the moment your pregnancy test is positive or don't show up until your baby is a few weeks old, don't beat yourself up when you aren't ecstatic all the time about having a baby.

Get together with another mommy-come-lately. Talk about your excitement, concerns, and questions.

Write your feelings in a journal. No one else ever needs to read what you express. My journal entries were a mix of "woe is me" and daydreaming about what my unborn child would be like.

Join the Late-in-Life Moms forum at www.mops.org or visit my website at www.MommyComeLately.com. Other late-in-life moms post questions and answers to the very things you wonder about.

Give yourself time. There were days when I tucked Christa in for a nap or read her books and wanted to ask, "What is a preschooler doing in my house?"

The Bottom Line

The mommies-come-lately I know have all learned to live with ambivalence. They realized life as a late-in-life mom is a strange mixture of exhaustion and exhilaration.

Choose some way to express your mixed feelings about your pregnancy. Confide in a trusted friend or write it all out in your journal.

Allow yourself time to adjust to your life as a mommy-come-lately.

Don't go it alone. Connect with other late-in-life moms.

═══ *Cameo Appearance:* **Vikki**

Repeater mommy-come-lately at forty-two

Husband: **Jack**

Children: **Michelle, age thirty-two; Matthew, age thirty-one; Jeremiah, age twenty-five; Jori, age eight**

Vikki said that since she had her first child very early in life, it didn't seem too strange to have her last one late in life.

"My husband and I were empty nesters when I got pregnant with Jori. We had visited friends—an older couple—who told us they were expecting. We congratulated them and later said, 'Can you imagine starting over at this age?' I think God thought, 'Oh, you think that's funny? Watch this!' Two weeks later, I got pregnant. I was forty-two and my husband was fifty-three."

Vikki responded to her late-in-life pregnancy with panic.

"I really didn't want a baby at that stage in my life. I had quit my job, had started a new career path, and was enjoying my freedom."

Her husband's response summed it up for them both: "I don't know whether to be really, really happy or cut my throat right now."

When Vikki called her then twenty-four-year-old daughter, it was almost comical to hear Michelle's daughter scream, "Grandma's going to have a baby!"

Vikki says, "I was healthier during that pregnancy than with my other three. I had dropped some weight and was eating very healthily. I actually glowed like I'd heard said so often about pregnant women."

Even so, Vikki went into preterm labor and delivered her daughter nine weeks early.

"I started bleeding at home, and my doctors wanted to put me in the hospital overnight for observation. I had just settled in when my water broke. Even though Jori weighed a small three pounds, everyone—even the Neonatal Intensive Care Unit (NICU) nurses—kept commenting on how great she looked for a preemie."

Jori was so young she didn't know how to suck. She remained in the NICU for almost a month so she could be fed through a tube until she learned how to suck. The doctors also kept her on oxygen for a week.

"There's really no point in second-guessing 'what if.' I prefer to leave the past in the past and live in the present with the hope of the future. I didn't realize having a child in my forties was my heart's desire, but God did."

Cameo Appearance: **Torie**

First-time mommy-come-lately at thirty-nine and again at forty-one and forty-three

Husband: **Joe**

Children: **Conor, age five and a half; Talbot, age four; Grace, age two and a half**

"I had a great career in the Air Force," Torie said. "I didn't meet my husband, Joe, until I was thirty-eight. It was worth waiting for my best friend. If you're dating, don't settle. Don't feel pressured if you get married later or start a family later," she said.

After getting married, Torie and Joe didn't want to wait to start a family. But, Torie added, "I also had seventeen years in the military, and I wanted to finish those last three years. Now, with three children, it is almost like those twenty years in the Air Force didn't exist."

Torie was an AMA mom for each of her pregnancies.

"I didn't understand every test the doctors did—and I always came up positive for whatever. The results were not going to change our decision to have a baby."

Torie's first two children, Conor and Talbot, were born with no health problems. Their daughter Grace, however, has Down syndrome. Torie said she knew it was a possibility because some of Grace's ultrasound measurements were off. Even so, she and Joe chose not to have amniocentesis.

"I do not introduce my daughter by saying, 'This is Grace, and she has Down syndrome.' I prayed for a healthy baby—

and she is healthy. Joe and I will deal with what we have to deal with—like the fact that Grace has mild hearing loss. She wears little purple and pink hearing aids."

While acknowledging that taking care of a special needs child is demanding, Torie said, "It can't all be about Grace. My other two children have their lives to live too.

"I love the naps when 'the stars are aligned' and all three little ones are asleep. I go lie down too. I'm learning to let go of things—and that's a big change. You have a plan, and if it doesn't work out, you learn to be flexible."

5

It Takes Two to Tango

Being an older dad is a great thing. You've experienced more of life before having kids. Bestow some of that experience on your children and give them that advantage.

> Steve, late-in-life dad at thirty-eight,
> almost forty, and forty-one

What about Dad? During a late-in-life pregnancy, the mom-to-be is center stage with the spotlight shining directly on her. Dad plays a supporting role in the production, catering to his wife's cravings, attending childbirth classes, and knowing his primary function is to coach his wife through labor and delivery.

But lots of adjustments are required of a man who becomes a father later in life. While he does not face the same physical risks that a mommy-come-lately does, he still navigates through many changes affecting his career and his family.

And the Award for Best Husband in a Supporting Role Goes To . . .

Early on, I didn't care how my unexpected pregnancy affected my husband. Rob's responsibility was to help me conquer my all-day morning sickness. He sliced lemons, ignored the cracker crumbs in our bed, and scrounged the local pharmacy for nausea remedies.

He also endured his medical colleagues asking, "Don't you know what causes pregnancy?" My dad even joked that it was all Rob's fault. A part of me wanted to agree. But the saying "It takes two to tango" was never truer. Besides, I didn't have the energy to lift my hand and point an accusing finger at Rob.

Well into my fourth month, my nausea dissipated and my emotional fog lifted. And I finally asked Rob, "How are you doing with all this?"

No response.

It was the end of a long day and we were lying in bed, so I thought maybe he had fallen asleep. Nope. I glanced over to see my husband just looking at me as if to say, "Are you talking to *me*?"

Rob seemed stunned to have any attention focused on him. He'd spent weeks pacing me as I mentally and physically wrestled with this pregnancy. If he'd now admitted to utter exhaustion, I wouldn't have been surprised.

"I was happy, but there was a part of me that was a little bit afraid," Rob recalled. "This certainly didn't fit in our plans. But more than that, I was concerned about how it was going to affect you and me. I was kind of waiting for you to whack me for getting you pregnant."

Better late than never, I realized my pregnancy threw Rob's life into upheaval too. He joked, "We saw light at the end of the tunnel—and it was an oncoming train."

As a physician, he knew the medical risks of a late-in-life pregnancy. As my husband, he also tried to maintain some semblance of a normal family life. He made omelets for dinner when I didn't feel like cooking. Or he picked up whatever type of food I craved that day. He ignored the messy house—and did laundry when he ran out of socks and underwear. He went to school meetings without making me feel guilty when I didn't have the get-up-and-go to attend.

Extreme Fatherhood

After Christa was born, Rob's escalating work problems further turned our life upside down. When Christa was seven months old, the Air Force stationed him two and a half hours away from home. Rob certainly never planned on being a *long distance* late-in-life dad.

Rob was used to having a short drive to work. The word "commute" took on a whole new, *exhausting* meaning with Rob driving back and forth from Colorado Springs to Wyoming. He usually left early Monday morning and came back home on Wednesday nights. Then he left early Thursday mornings and came back for the weekends. His being away from home for days at a time added additional stress on the whole family.

Deprived of seeing Christa on a daily basis, when he was home Rob insisted on putting Christa to bed. He often fell asleep in the rocking chair with her in his arms.

"You know, you're establishing a habit here," I warned him, worried about Christa getting used to being held until she fell asleep each night.

"Yeah, but it's okay. This is our special time together," Rob replied. To this day Christa enjoys—and expects—extra bedtime snuggles with her dad. And if she wakes up in the middle of the night, she comes looking for him—not me.

Even before Christa was born, Rob was concerned about losing our freedom—our ability to have time together. Some of our friends were emptying their nests. They enjoyed having time for each other again. As one couple we knew discussed plans for a romantic cruise, Rob and I just looked at each other. What could we say except, "We're envious." There were no cruise plans in our near future. When we finally do take our still-delayed twenty-fifth anniversary cruise, Christa's older siblings will provide child care!

But Rob refused to concentrate on what we lost when Christa was born. He said, "It's easy to fall into the mind-set of 'Oh, we're not going to be able to do the things we wanted to do.' It's somewhat of a selfish mentality. God gave us Christa not so she can tag along with our life. She has a life of her own."

Rob's major focus was remembering how to connect with a toddler. During the time our three older children were embarking to high school, college, and careers, Christa was progressing from diapers and occasional naps to learning to eat with a fork.

"I was used to attending soccer matches and band concerts and wrestling tournaments," Rob said. "I had to consciously think, *What would a preschooler like to do?* I had to be willing to take a walk to the park and let her swing on the swings or roll down the hill—and carry her home when she was tired."

Christa made Rob rethink his priorities. Our teenagers didn't require as much time and effort as a preschooler. At a point when he could have invested more time into his military career, Rob opted to retire. In a very real way, Christa rearranged our priorities. Rob weighed his career against the needs of his

His, Mine, and Ours

Wendy remarried when she was twenty-six and had a three-year-old daughter. Her husband, Mike, was thirty-nine and had a teenage daughter.

"To be honest, both of us were straddling the fence about having another child," Wendy said, adding that their two children were already adjusting to a lot of change. "Apparently we had too much fun while straddling the fence on this decision. Within a few short weeks of our honeymoon blurring into the day-to-day life of our marriage, we found out that I was pregnant with 'ours.'"

When Andrew was born, their oldest daughter was sixteen and their youngest daughter was four.

"Parenting such broad age ranges has been a lesson in survival and sanity," Wendy said. "Parenting is never easy, but when your children are closer in age, at least you have the benefit of built-in playmates and somewhat similar routines, needs, and activities."

Wendy also said that "parenting at extremes" creates a strong sense of the need to do right by each child that can be mind-boggling. In the course of one twenty-four-hour period, Wendy

- helped their oldest daughter get ready to go to college
- made a list of school supplies needed by their middle daughter, who was starting first grade
- changed numerous diapers, watched Elmo, and read books to their toddler

"As the parent of a blended family, you have to rise above your limitations and pray—pray a lot," Wendy said. "Somehow, through grace, we handle being the parents of the kids God gave us. Another day goes by and our youngest does something new. Our middle child does something new. Our oldest does something new. Every day we are renewed as parents.

"Do my husband and I plan on having any more children now that he is south of forty and I am almost past thirty? Not really. Well, we don't know. Maybe. Maybe not. The debate continues as the biological clocks keep ticking."

family—including a toddler—and decided to pursue a career option that did not require travel and constant moving. Our first three children grew up as "military brats," adjusting to moves that uprooted them from friends and schools. Christa will have little remembrance of her dad's military days.

The Best Adventure of All

Even though Doug Darr didn't get married until he was thirty-nine, he still considered having kids.

"It wasn't out of the question. I'd never been around kids, but even so, there was some interest. Then, as time went on and Mary didn't get pregnant, I started thinking maybe it wasn't going to happen. I'm career minded. I would be okay if we couldn't have kids."

When Mary complained about not feeling well, Doug wondered if she might be pregnant, but he didn't say anything. He came home from work one day to find Mary sitting on the edge of the couch, waiting for him.

"I thought, *Here we go . . .*" Doug said.

Mary's pregnancy at forty-six created conflicting emotions for Doug. "Life was going to be different. I don't know if I was excited or apprehensive," Doug said with a laugh. "I don't know what I was.

"I started hearing about the risks for women her age—and yes, I was worried. Then I decided it didn't matter. What we got, we got. I believed we were going to be fine from the beginning. Deep down in my gut I knew it was going to be fine."

Mary's ultrasound early in her pregnancy confirmed Doug's optimism.

"Everyone was saying, 'See this, see that?' And I didn't see anything they were talking about. Finally, I saw a tiny blip. When I asked what it was, they said, 'Let's turn the sound up'—and I heard the baby's heartbeat. I was hooked. It was perfect."

Doug recalled the stress created by Mary's interaction with her first ob-gyn: "He came highly recommended. I guess he thought he was doing what he should be doing. But Mary felt he was threatening what she believed—and threatening her child. Our mind-set about potential problems was that it didn't matter. My role was to be supportive of my wife."

After Mary's twenty-plus hour labor and delivery, Doug didn't get home from the hospital until midnight. On his way home he stopped and collected the mail. Flipping through the bills and advertisements, he opened a blue envelope. Inside? His American Association of Retired Persons (AARP) card.

"I'd turned fifty years old two weeks earlier. People at work called me 'Grandpa' and asked, 'Did you decide to have the grandkids before you had kids?'"

Because of the complications with Mary's epidural, she spent the first five days after Justin's birth lying flat on her back. With the help of the nurses, Doug took care of his newborn son.

"I'd never been around a baby. Nobody prepared me for this. I'd run home and sleep and run back to the hospital and then run home again."

He relied on the basic skills he'd learned while attending the "Baby Boot Camp" that Mary had encouraged him to attend. And, yes, once again Doug was the oldest dad there. "I could have been the father of some of the younger guys," he said.

Doug believes being a late-in-life dad has advantages: "I've watched other guys do it. When Justin was born, I knew what I wanted to do and what I didn't want to do as a dad. I had the ability to adjust my job schedule, and I'm better prepared financially. You can't have a footloose and fancy-free life and raise kids. I've had that, so I am more settled, more satisfied with who I am.

"I am now a family man, but I still have an independent piece in my head. I have career goals I'm pursuing. I still want to travel. But every day I look forward to going home because Justin and our dog race each other to the door to meet me. And that is the better part of my day."

Justin also insists on another father-son tradition.

"When I leave for work, I have to flash the headlights or honk—if it's not too early in the morning—or switch on the police lights," Doug said with a smile.

"All the things I like were replaced by something I like more—my son. I have to believe God orchestrated my life, including the timing of Justin's birth. God knew what I needed. I've done a ton of things. I've been on my adventures. This one is the best of all."

An Experienced Perspective: Looking Back on Late-in-Life Fatherhood

Mike is on the opposite end of late-in-life fatherhood from Rob and Doug. His son Matthew—now nine-

> *I want to be working less when my kids are teenagers so I can spend a lot of time with them. I want to be there for them. I've analyzed what other people have done. As a parent, you have to be there. You can't be too busy.*
>
> Steven, late-in-life dad at thirty-seven, thirty-nine, and forty-one

Some Facts on Male Infertility

A recent study in the *Journal of the American Medical Association (JAMA)* found a man's fertility begins declining at age thirty-five—not in his forties and fifties as previously believed. As men age, they also produce more sperm with genetic defects. In 40 to 50 percent of infertile couples, sperm are the problem. The most common cause of infertility in men who have already had children is a varicocele—an enlarged vein in the testicle that increases heat and interferes with both sperm and hormone production.

The good news is there are major medical advances for couples undergoing in vitro fertilization (IVF) because of male infertility. Doctors can inject one healthy sperm directly into the woman's egg using intracytoplasmic sperm injection (ICSI).

"Medical Implications of the Male Biological Clock," *JAMA* Vol. 296, No. 19, November 15, 2006

teen years old—was born when Mike was forty and his wife, Margo, was almost forty-one.

For seventeen years Mike and Margo battled the emotional and physical ups and downs of infertility.

"We explored every facet of infertility to the maximum limit of medical technology at that time," Mike said. "We got no satisfaction from all the medical testing."

The joy of their long-hoped-for pregnancy was overshadowed by Margo spending six months on complete bed rest under the specter of miscarrying.

"Both Margo and I knew we would love our child," Mike said. "But it caught us pleasantly by surprise that we would 'fall in love' with him. Especially in the early years, I couldn't wait to get home to see what new things he learned or did—what memory-making comments he'd made during the day."

Mike believes that because they were older, he and Margo appreciated Matthew more than if he had arrived earlier in their marriage.

Late-in-Life Fathers' Perspectives

Better to be a late-in-life dad than no dad at all.

> Joe, late-in-life dad at thirty-six, thirty-eight, and forty

Focus on the benefits that a late-in-life parent can bring to the game. It's a bit like a veteran relief pitcher in baseball who comes in late in the game and uses all his experience and wisdom to bring home a win for the team. He wouldn't want to go back and be a twentysomething starting pitcher who still makes a lot of rookie mistakes and sometimes costs the team a game because of it.

> Dave K., late-in-life dad at age forty-two

There was concern about what this would do to our family—and there was happiness about what this would do to our family.

> Rob, repeater late-in-life dad at forty-three

The prevailing attitude of men my age is that this should be a time to enjoy life and the fruits of your past labor. But I don't intend to retire. I fully expect to be active with my children through their teen years and beyond. I look forward to that.

> Doug W., late-in-life dad by adoption at forty-five and again at forty-eight

Get ready because your life is going to be turned upside down—and you're going to love it!

> Doug D., first-time late-in-life dad at fifty

I want to keep up with the culture Christa's growing up in so I can be relevant. I want to speak words she can hear.

> Rob, repeater late-in-life dad at forty-three

Spending time with my son was not a requirement but a privilege. Talking and playing with him was not "the right thing to do," it was a major reason for getting up in the morning.

> Mike, late-in-life dad at forty

It's a little scary when you realize getting down on the floor and playing with your children is no longer an option.

> Dr. Kevin Leman, repeater late-in-life dad at forty-four and forty-nine

I am at a time in my life when I can really enjoy my child. I've accomplished about all I'm going to accomplish; I'm at the pinnacle. The only thing I have to do is spend enough time with my daughter—and enjoy her. I hope she remembers me and enjoys me.

> Dave S., late-in-life adoptive dad at forty-eight

"I may have taken him for granted as someone who was a 'natural by-product of loving one another' rather than knowing he is a special gift from God. We readily saw his creation and health as 'answered prayer' and happily and soberly accepted our responsibility to raise him."

A Tradition of Love

Mike established a tradition eighteen years ago when Matthew was an infant. Here is how he described it:

From the time Matthew was born up until he left for college, I wrote down on a scrap piece of paper little events in his life or something he said that was either funny or a milestone of some kind. I put those pieces of paper in a safe place. Once a year—as close to his birthday as possible—I took the scraps out, sequenced them chronologically, and then used them as "memory joggers" or talking points as I made an audiotape from me to him. I went through all those memories—quite often tearfully or with a crackling voice—highlighting them for him.

Because I was older than the normal "little kid dad," I viewed each annual tape as the last one I might be able to make. So I always took the last part of the tape to tell him about how much I love him and my hopes that he develop in Christ.

I then duplicated the tape and stored one set at home and one set at the office in case of fire. (Now with the new CD technology, I am having the tapes put onto CDs—and will have two sets made.) Matthew does not know that I have done this. Even though he is eighteen, I am not sure he can fully appreciate them. My plan is to give them to him either as a wedding present or a few weeks before his first child is born.

Doing this has been a great source of memories for me—and over time, an unspoken commitment to Matthew.

Dave S., Adoptive Dad at Forty-eight

Dave S. says his view of adopting his daughter Tori is different than his wife's experience. (Linda's story is told in chapter 1.)

"I was sympathetic to the issues of an open adoption, but I don't know that I had the same emotions that my wife Linda had," Dave said. "For one thing, Linda developed a stronger relationship with the birth mom. Because Linda was almost the same age as the woman's mom, she developed a motherly kind of relationship with her."

"It's awkward for men to get involved in something like this. It is more of a female-to-female thing. I just tried to be supportive," Dave said.

Adopting Tori was not an easy experience. When the birth father kept Tori after a visitation, refusing to return her to her birth mother, Dave and Linda agreed they needed to help the birth mom.

"I told the birth mom I would make everything right— whatever it cost. I hired an attorney and said we would help her get control of the situation and insist that the birth father pay child support," Dave said.

Once both birth parents decided to proceed with letting Dave and Linda adopt Tori, Dave focused on supporting Linda.

"During the last week of those ninety days, Linda wanted to get away. She didn't want to be at home waiting for a phone call. She didn't want to take the phone call if either parent changed their mind," Dave recalled. He rented a place in the mountains, getting up at 3:00 a.m. to get ready for work and drive to his job two and a half hours away.

"I was the manager of my department, so I could do what I wanted, pretty much. I would get into work by 6:30 a.m. and work until 3:30 p.m. Then I'd finish work via my cell phone while driving back up the mountain."

After they passed the ninety-day mark, they spoke to the social worker. She told them, "Yes, the waiting period is over, but until you get the signed adoption papers, there is still some risk." It was another two or three months until the adoption was final.

Dave said that at forty-eight, he was excited about becoming a dad and that being older did not bother him. "I thought it would be a lot of fun—very interesting and challenging. Financially, I was comfortable. I was older, so I wasn't going out at night. I could devote time to my family. I could appreciate my daughter."

Dave's three younger brothers were all adopted, so Dave understands that Tori may want to meet her birth mother some day. He says, "Each individual treats it differently. One of my brothers was always interested in learning about his birth mom. When he wasn't able to connect with her, he was troubled by it. However, my other brothers didn't care. If Tori wants to meet her birth mom, then it is going to happen. At twelve, Tori is such a grounded girl, and she has a great value system. She isn't going to think, 'Oh, this is my mom now.'"

Dave mentioned only one thing he felt was a drawback for Tori because she has older parents: his parents are in their nineties and live in an assisted-living facility. "Tori has grandparents in name only. She has a sense of responsibility about seeing them—trying to get to know them and understand who they are. But she doesn't visit her grandparents for the same reason I visited mine—to get what I couldn't get at home."

As he talked about his daughter, Dave summed up all his feelings by saying, "When Tori was a baby, I looked at her—and then I realized I fell in love with her just looking at her."

Dave K., Late-in-Life Dad at Forty-two

When his thirty-six-year-old wife Lisa was pregnant, Dave's concerns went beyond her mommy-come-lately status. Dave also wondered how her pregnancy would affect her lupus, an autoimmune disorder.

"One doctor mentioned to us that a pregnancy can sometimes act as a 'reset button' for people who have connective tissue disease. So we were somewhat hopeful that there could be a positive outcome for Lisa in addition to the blessing of our daughter, Rachel," Dave said. "As it was, Lisa's symptoms got worse both during and after the pregnancy." Even so, he said, Lisa's pregnancy was the fulfillment of a lifelong dream.

Dave sees many advantages to being an older parent: "Lisa and I are a bit wiser than we would have been in our twenties. We have a more mature, selfless approach to parenting. It's not as hard to give up some of the things we used to do—like travel, watching football together on Sunday afternoons, or going out on dates—in order to enjoy time with Rachel. I think those priorities would have been more difficult to adjust to earlier in life."

Dave also appreciates his financial security and the maturity of his faith. "These things allow me to focus more on being a dad for Rachel—and hopefully to pass on some of the positives while shielding her from the negatives. I also have the ability to be somewhat detached when disciplining Rachel. I think the extra experience in years allows me to see past the heat of the moment and beyond to the positive outcome.

"The age factor is sometimes a bit hard to take. I'm not sure whether I'll be around for milestones like her wedding and her first child or adult problems and situations she might need advice on. I don't like to think that she'll most likely be around for many years without me. I have some regrets that Rachel may need me at some time that younger fathers would normally be there for—so it creates a bit of a negative for her life as well. If I stop to think about it too long, it makes me sad."

Dave said he and Lisa decided there is a "melancholy factor" for older parents: "Although we see the present clearer than we might have as a younger mom and dad, the future also seems more tangible somehow. Thoughts of Rachel growing up, dating, going off to college, and getting married are all hard to accept while we are still in the phase where we are her whole world. I think as younger parents, we'd probably be so focused on getting through each day and growing up ourselves that the future would seem pretty distant—and more naturally acceptable."

A New Spin on Fatherhood

Being a late-in-life dad puts a whole new spin on the challenge of fatherhood.

"Someone says, 'Pretty soon you're going to have an empty nest.' Yeah, when I'm seventy-one. It's just fact. That's the way it is. But I wouldn't change a thing," said Dr. Kevin Leman, a well-known author and speaker on family issues.

Dr. Leman is a late-in-life dad twice over. His children are thirty-four, thirty-two, twenty-nine, nineteen, and fourteen. He and his wife Sande reacted to their first late-in-life child with "absolute glee," he said. "We had three kids—and now we get to do it again!"

With their second caboose baby—number five—he kept saying, "*What? What?* We'd had our surprise child. We were forty-seven and forty-nine. Adjusting to that one took about three weeks of me walking around and talking to myself. To this day I call her my little gift from God—and she knows it."

"You do the math," Dr. Leman said. "I'm near death and I've got a fourteen-year-old. Just staying alive long enough to watch them grow up and become who they're supposed to become is a challenge."

Dr. Leman likes to look for a chance to slip his kids "commercial announcements"—or words of encouragement.

You Do the Math

All the older parents I've met "do the math" just like Dr. Leman said. They calculate their child's milestones not just based on how old their child will be—but based on how old they will be too. Late-in-life pregnancy prompts all sorts of mental mathematical gymnastics as Mom and Dad grasp the reality—in days, months, and years—of how life is changed by a baby's arrival.

Rob and I have done our own calculations since Christa's arrival. Mathematically speaking, our future looks something like this:

1. When my daughter Amy began college, Christa started kindergarten.

2. While Rob and I fight midlife spread, Christa will be reveling in the kids' menu—including free dessert!

3. When Rob and I qualify for our AARP cards at age fifty, we will be chaperoning elementary school field trips.

4. When Christa hits puberty, I will be postmenopausal. Now *that* we like!

5. When Christa graduates from high school, I will be sixty. Rob will be sixty-two.

6. When Christa celebrates turning eighteen, her older brother Josh will be thirty-six. Katie Beth will be thirty-three. Amy will be thirty-one. Three *really, really, really* adult children—and a teenager!

7. As Christa grows up, my just-for-fun blonde highlights will become a desperate attempt to cover my gray hair so I am not mistaken for her grandmother.

8. Rob's retirement is pushed back by at least a decade, replaced with building a college fund for Christa.

9. When we qualify for a senior-citizen discount, Christa will be eligible for a student discount.

"I tell them, 'I know I'm old and near death, but this is what I see going on in your life—and it seems like you're handling life well.'"

Dr. Leman laughingly recalled walking his youngest daughter into her classroom. Another man passed by him and said, "I've got a grandchild in this school too."

"Actually, this is number five," Dr. Leman replied.

"Oh? Five grandchildren! Aren't you lucky!"

"And with that I just kept on walking. It ain't worth it. You just have to let them think what they want to think," he said.

He encourages other late-in-life dads to enjoy the ride. Whether you are a first-time dad at forty-seven or experience a caboose baby, "Try to be as involved as you possibly can be," he said. "How you handle it is going to make a big difference in how the whole family handles it."

The Bottom Line

Dads have a vital role in parenting—and often a different perspective from moms on having children later in life.

Strive to be relevant in your child's life. Stay involved with their interests, their activities, and the culture in which they are growing up.

Make time to start a tradition like recording special memories of your child in a journal or on a digital voice recorder. You'll be giving your son or daughter a precious gift.

Cameo Appearance: **Paul**

First-time late-in-life dad at forty and again at forty-two

Wife: **Elizabeth**

Children: **Tommy, age seven; Ellie, age five**

Paul and his wife Elizabeth were married for ten years before starting a family.

"We knew when we got married that we would eventually have children. But people started to nag us immediately about it. So, to get them to leave us alone, we feigned a high level of indifference—and it worked," Paul said. "That freed us up to start our family when we believed it was the right time for us, rather than when others expected it."

As the years went by, Paul said he was aware of his age.

"I didn't want to be an old father—and I knew as I approached forty that I was teetering on the edge of being comfortable with my age as a father. My wife is seven years younger than me, so the timing for her was entirely different."

Elizabeth is from England, and in 1991 they moved back overseas, planning to make England their permanent home. The timing seemed right, so both Paul and Elizabeth decided they were ready to pursue having children. Within a few months, Elizabeth was pregnant.

Paul recalls his "vivid reaction" to Elizabeth's announcement that she was pregnant.

"Elizabeth had done a pregnancy test, which was positive, but we decided we wouldn't tell anyone immediately. At the time I was a freelance writer and would often go into the town near our home and do some writing at a local cafe. I remember vividly walking to the cafe, and I had this feeling of walking on air. I wanted to tell passing strangers, 'Hi, I'm going to be a father.' It was elation—I don't know of any other feeling I've ever had like that—joy."

Their son Tommy was born in 1999. Despite their original plans to settle in England, Paul and Elizabeth moved back to the States when Tommy was a year old. Then, a year later during a visit to Elizabeth's parents back in England, Elizabeth found out she was pregnant again.

"That had a kind of poetry to it—to learn we were having our second baby while we were in England. We were thrilled."

Their daughter Ellie was born in 2001.

When asked about being an older dad, Paul recounts a line from the television show M*A*S*H.

"Radar was talking about how his father was so much older and had a heart attack the first time they played peek-a-boo. I used that same joke after my two children were born. And I often tease my kids when I've run out of energy that it's their fault for having an older father."

Like many later-in-life dads, Paul thinks there is a distinct advantage to being forty and forty-two when his children were born.

"I'm inclined to think I would have made more mistakes as a younger dad. I'm not a perfect parent, but I don't think I'm making as many mistakes as I might have made in my impetuous youth. Being older has tempered me a bit."

6

One for All—and All for the Little One

Christa reminds me to have fun — to still play "tea party" and dress up and to believe in fairy tales again.

Christa's nineteen-year-old sister, Amy

Christa's older siblings have their own perspectives on our now six-year-old experience of Christa — or "Sugarplum" or "'Twas" or "Loo-Hoo" or "Boo" — depending on the nicknames doled out by the older kids. Dr. Leman says you don't get to name your kid when there are older siblings around. You don't have proprietary rights on terms of endearment either. But when Amy wanted to name Christa "Bambi," Rob and I vetoed the idea — despite her insistence that it was in our book of baby names.

Initially I hoped our fourth child would be a boy, thinking it would help Josh connect more easily with his much-younger sibling. Unfazed by our "It's a girl!" announcement, Josh assured me all was well, saying, "It's not like I spent the last sixteen years wishing for a brother."

After Christa's holiday birth, the kids stayed with us in the birthing center and traipsed along when I transferred to a private room. We have a family tradition of opening presents on Christmas Eve—and we kept it, albeit on a much smaller scale. After a quick trip home, Josh brought a few presents back to the hospital. While Christa slept snuggled in the blanket her sisters had made for her, we opened gifts. Then the three older kids headed home and Christa, Rob, and I settled in for the night.

I talk with Christa about my guy problems. I'll say, "So, Christa, there's these two boys . . . what should I do?" She says, "Go with the nice guy." Christa makes everything simple.

Amy, nineteen years old

It's not always easy. I don't always know how to relate to Emily. Not seeing her all the time, I don't always recognize how much she has grown up.

Beth J., thirty years old

Whether you see yourself as a role model or not, you become one. Christa mimics me and Amy all the time.

Katie Beth, twenty-one years old

What do you do with a much-younger sibling? Having the goal to have a good relationship with her is always a good start.

Josh, twenty-four years old

I wouldn't go back to life before Christa. In some ways it would be easier—less responsibility. But I also know she's made everything better. She is here for a reason.

Amy, nineteen years old

The only conflicts are that Mama and Dad are still busy with childrearing themselves and cannot be free to help as much as we would hope with our kids. Being Grandma comes second to being Mama.

Rachel M., thirty years old

I wasn't called on to babysit too often, but the baby was such a novelty to my friends that I ended up taking her with me a lot anyway. From my parents' perspective, Emily must have been a great chaperone to send on my dates.

Beth J., thirty years old

The next day was the first Christmas that Rob and I were separated from Josh, Katie Beth, and Amy. Getting discharged from the hospital was a whole lot more challenging than when my first three children were born. Rob and I were required to watch a basic child-care video and one on proper car seat installation. There was no going home until we'd viewed both from start to finish—with the girls calling every hour on the hour to ask, "When are you bringing Christa home?"

The Christmas holidays provided extra time for Christa with her siblings. They took turns holding her, snuggling with her in the same rocking chair that I'd used to rock each one of them.

In the early months, Christa just adapted to her siblings' schedules. She went to wrestling meets to "watch" Josh compete. On parents' night, Josh presented me with a rose—and his teammates presented Christa with a Bible storybook and a stuffed frog. She became the team's mascot.

Through the years she also danced her way through her sisters' choir and band concerts—and kicked her pink soccer ball along the sidelines during Amy's games. When I picked up the girls from school, they liked to show off Christa to their friends—stealing her out of her car seat and strolling around the hallways with her.

Each one of her older siblings had their own idea of how things would go once Christa joined the family. Josh stated his goal clearly: "I want to be able to tell Christa that I never changed her diaper."

That sounded reasonable, but I felt like we needed to reach some sort of compromise. Josh had an amazing and oh-so-appreciated knack for getting Christa to sleep when she was fussy. My proposition: no diaper duty *if* Josh would settle her down when I couldn't. One of Josh's strongest memories is walking around his bedroom holding his infant sister until his pacing and the Celtic music in the background lulled Christa to sleep. His mantra for his little sister was "No fussing, no crying."

Katie Beth is the "mommy" big sister. Amy is the "fun" big sister. Katie Beth didn't mind changing diapers—well, if she did, she didn't complain. When Christa was a toddler, Katie Beth made sure her little sister brushed her teeth and went to bed on time. Katie Beth was so good at the mom routine that I had to remind her that I was the mom, not her.

Amy was a pushover when it came to Christa's bedtimes. If Christa fussed, Amy took her out of her crib and brought her back downstairs. And it was Amy who donned her bathing suit and played in the tub with Christa. She took all the cushions off the couch and piled them into a fort for Christa to crawl over and under and all around. Amy tolerated Christa grabbing and yanking on her long, long hair. She also dressed her in fun outfits and held impromptu photo shoots.

Dr. Kevin Leman on Siblings

"With adult children around, all of a sudden they think they're having a child," Dr. Leman said. "They think they get to have equal input. Everybody rallies around the little ones, and everyone is concerned about the little ones. The siblings become like surrogate parents."

Then Dr. Leman corrected himself: "It's not so much surrogate parenting. I think what they are doing is becoming good brothers and sisters. Parents step back and let that happen." Then he laughed and said, "I wouldn't say 'step back' is the right term. 'Failure to get out of the chair' is more accurate."

Dr. Leman understood that Christa is a confusing mix of fourth child, baby, firstborn, and only child.

"She should be more of a firstborn personality," Dr. Leman said. "Her older siblings will look at her as the mascot, the baby. But as Christa grows, you'll see more firstborn tendencies. She'll get along with adults better than with kids her own age."

When Josh left home for college, I worried he and Christa would not know one another.

"I don't know what your relationship with Christa will be like—but it's important you have some type of relationship with her," I said.

Five years later, Josh is Christa's hero.

"I love Josh more than anybody in the whole world," Christa proclaimed.

"Even more than me?" I asked.

"Yes," she replied with no sense of guilt. She thinks Josh is a superhero and that he can pick up cars à la Mr. Incredible.

Christa has two mommies. There's Katie Beth—and then there's that other mommy.

Christa's preschool friend Jack's announcement to his daddy

Josh, Katie Beth, and Amy all see past the "fun" of Christa and acknowledge their position of influence in her life.

"Realizing I have to act like a responsible role model is tons of pressure," Josh admitted. At the same time he likes the absence of the sibling squabbles he participated in with Katie Beth and Amy—competing for the same toys, their parents' attention, and the front seat in the car.

"Because of the time Christa spends with me and Amy, she seems like a little walking teenager," Katie Beth said. "But she can't have the same experiences as a teenager. My relationship with Christa is so different from my relationship with Josh and Amy. I'm not the mom—I get to have more fun. But I am a role model."

Amy admits, "I watch what I say and do because she wants to be like me. I try to influence her spiritually. If she's scared, I'll say, 'Let's pray.'"

Both Amy and Katie Beth have been mistaken for Christa's mother. The first week we took Christa to church, Katie Beth

Long-Distance Sibling Relationships

1. If you're the away-from-home older sibling, don't just call your mother. Call your younger sister or brother.

2. Use the Internet. Instant message (IM) your younger sibling. (Parents, let your caboose baby IM her older brothers and sisters—even if her messages look like "zzztttiiioooo." Teach her how to send a "sticker" using emoticons. Invest in a Web camera and a microphone so siblings can see and hear each other.)

3. Take some of your family's photos and put them up around your dorm room or apartment as a visual reminder to keep in touch with your sibling.

4. Go the extra mile and travel to see your younger sibling. (Parents, when possible, provide the money for a plane ticket to bring older siblings home. It's not just an expense—it's an investment.) If possible, invite your younger brother or sister to visit you.

5. Good, old-fashioned "snail mail" is a special treat for a younger sibling. Drop a card or handwritten letter in the mail.

held her as we sat down. Two older women sitting in front of us turned and looked at Katie Beth. They gave her a disapproving stare and then whispered to one another. I realized they thought Katie Beth was an unwed, teenage mom.

"Take the baby away from Katie Beth. You hold her," Amy whispered to me.

"No. If those women are going to think the worst—in front of God and everybody—that's their problem."

Another time, Katie Beth was walking with a then four-year-old Christa in the mall. A group of teenage girls walked by—and then shouted, "Stay in school!"

Both girls have learned to take it in stride. I even bought Christa two identical T-shirts that say "I'm the little sister" on them. But I also told the girls Christa couldn't wear these shirts every day of the week.

When we're out together, I often try to designate who's who. I'll make sure the cashier knows I'm the mom by telling Christa to "Hold Mommy's hand"—and then reaching out for her. Or I'll tell her to catch up to her sisters while we're walking in the mall—usually saying it loud enough for others to hear. That way maybe we won't get so many stares from curious shoppers.

Not the Classic Siblings

Remember Karen's story from chapter 2? Her oldest daughter Beth is now thirty and has plenty of experience as a much older sibling to her sister Emily. Beth remembered that people always assumed that Emily was her baby and that their mother was Emily's grandmother.

> *My husband and I had picked out two names. If it was a boy, either Nathan or Aaron. We finally decided on Nathan. But when his teenage brothers saw the baby for the first time, they told us, "He looks like an Aaron." We called him Aaron instead.*
>
> Janet, mommy-come-lately at thirty-five

"Whether it was the waitress in the restaurant or the photographer at the photo studio, people would always direct their questions to me. I always thought it was funny. Fortunately, so did my mom. My husband is still getting used to it," Beth said.

"Emily and I are not classic siblings. I am on some sort of pedestal, the distant treat who shows up a couple of times a year. I'm trendier and cooler than parents, but I'm still an adult."

Creating a good relationship with Emily took time and effort.

"When Emily was younger, I would always tuck her in and sing to her when I was in town. I would practice my songs for choir, sing praise songs, sing top 40 songs, whatever came into my head. There were lots of songs. We spent the first five years singing one thing or another."

One particular tune sung at bedtime became their song. "It became our 'sister song,'" Beth said. "I wanted her to know that we had a different, special, giant kind of bond, even if I was almost never around."

Beth also said her parents did everything they could to help her and Emily stay connected.

"When I went away to college, they made sure that Emily took her turns to talk to me on the phone. As a preschooler, Emily had a world map on her wall. They would move a pin around to show her where I was—at college, traveling for debate team events, visiting friends, or spending a summer in Europe."

But Beth also said her parents didn't push the relationship. She never felt like there were many expectations or sacrifices she had to make.

"My sixteenth birthday was five days after Emily was born. Yet I got to have my birthday. My dad drove me and my best friend to the beach and disappeared for the day, then came back out to buy us dinner on the boardwalk, and then disappeared again so we could hang out for the evening.

"I work hard to have a relationship with her—though not always as hard as I should. I call home more often than I would if it were just my parents. When I am home, Emily is my first priority. I make the time for her because I know it's limited. We do 'sister trips' with just us. Wherever she wants to go—shopping, movies, this past year it was Starbucks."

For many years, Beth and Emily had "the Speech"—delivered at the end of each phone call, regardless of whether it was bedtime or not. The sisters alternated phrases, with Beth starting a sentence and Emily finishing it:

> Good / night
> Sleep / tight
> Don't let any / bedbugs bite
> But if they / do
> Hit 'em with a / shoe
> And always remember
> *THAT I LOVE YOU!* (said together and *loud*)

One Is the Loneliest Number—or Not

Sometimes I feel guilty that Christa does not have a sister or brother closer to her age. In some ways, she lives the life of an only child.

"Only children do extremely well in life," according to Dr. Leman. "Unnecessary guilt trips are placed on moms. I don't think many men get that. People say all kinds of stupid things. Just ignore it."

In his well-known book *The Birth Order Book*, Dr. Leman takes a "good news, bad news" approach to only children. He says, "The only child has a unique advantage/disadvantage: He or she has never had to compete with siblings for parental attention, favor, or resources" (Grand Rapids: Revell, 2004, 130).

While an only child is often confident, articulate, and on top of things, never having to deal with brothers or sisters can cause him to be "self-centered by default," Dr. Leman said.

There are two types of "Onlies," according to Dr. Leman. There are the "Special Jewels," where the parents wanted more

Look Who Is an Only Child

When Linda's daughter, Tori, was younger, she kept saying she wanted a brother or a sister. Linda told Tori she was too old to adopt another child and encouraged her to be realistic about having siblings.

"I have all my time for you," Linda said. "You are the only one we want. We love you, and you are the one we are spending our time on."

As an only child, Tori is in good company with other successful "Onlies," including:

Robin Williams, comedian
Natalie Portman, actress
Rudy Giuliani, former mayor of New York City
Tipper Gore, political activist and wife of former vice president Al Gore
Lillian Hellman, playwright
Kareem Abdul-Jabbar, professional basketball player
Franklin Delano Roosevelt, former president
Alan Greenspan, former Federal Reserve Board chairman
Cary Grant, actor
Frank Sinatra, singer
Lauren Bacall, actress
Cole Porter, songwriter
Dick Cavett, television talk show host
Robert De Niro, actor
William Randolph Hearst, newspaper publisher and politician
James Michener, author
Roger Staubach, pro-football quarterback
Van Cliburn, concert pianist
Elizabeth Bishop, poet
Burt Bacharach, singer, songwriter

www.onlychild.com

children but only had one. When the parents devote all their time and attention to this child, he may feel overly important. And if the only child arrives when the parents are older, he can become the center of their universe.

According to Dr. Leman, there are also the "Parental Plan" Onlies, where the parents planned on one child. Often they grow up in a very structured, disciplined environment and are treated like a little adult. With so much time and attention focused on them, Onlies can become ultraperfectionists. Dr. Leman's advice: "Lower the high jump bar on your life" (p. 146). In other words, don't demand perfection from yourself or your child.

The Bottom Line

Talk with your older children about developing a relationship with their much-younger brother or sister. And then help them establish a connection by

taking advantage of the Internet and the telephone,

thanking them when they take the time to read to or play with their sibling,

reminding them of the important role they have in their sibling's life, and

developing their own traditions, like taking their younger sister or brother out for ice cream or singing a special song together.

Cameo Appearance: **Ann**

Repeater mommy-come-lately at thirty-seven and again at forty

Husband: **Marv**

Children: **Colin, age thirty-four; Cameron, age thirty; Miriam, age twenty-two; Samuel, age nineteen**

Ann always wanted two children, so she was satisfied after her son Colin and her daughter Cameron were born. When her husband Marv asked her if she wanted any more children, she said no. But when he asked her to pray about it, she agreed.

"When I didn't get pregnant, I said, 'Thank you for agreeing with me, God.' Then after I had a miscarriage, I had the desire to have more children," Ann said.

During separate times of prayer, both Ann and Marv felt God impress on them that they would have a son. Like the biblical story of Samuel, who grew up to be an Old

Testament priest, both of them believed God said their son-
to-be Samuel would be God's servant. Three years later,
when her daughter Miriam was born, Ann wondered when
God would accomplish what he had said.

Three years later, she was pregnant again. But the baby
wasn't growing properly. Then, during her sixth month, a
sonogram picked up an abnormality.

"There was fluid in the baby's abdomen, and we were told
this indicated some sort of major organ problem," Ann said.
After friends and family prayed for the baby, a follow-up test
revealed that every drop of fluid was gone.

Samuel was born on Miriam's third birthday, weighing
only 5 pounds 12 ounces. Before his birth, they did not know
if he had Down syndrome or not.

"There was a pall over the delivery room," Ann recalled.
"And then Marv came in and told me they were pretty
sure Samuel had Down syndrome. I began a deep grieving
process. We thought the Lord's servant would be a pastor or
an evangelist or a missionary—not this. It was the loss of a
dream."

The delivery room was quiet when Sam was born. "Marv
took little Sam in his arms and held him close. He hoped
that gesture would convey to our son that he would be loved
and cared for," Ann said.

As she recalled her struggle to accept Sam's Down
syndrome, Ann talked about reading a letter in the National
Down Syndrome Association newsletter. Another mother of
a Down syndrome child described her experience like this:
"They say it is like a person planning a trip to Italy—and then
ending up in Holland. You have to change your perspective.
Italy is beautiful—but so is Holland, in a different way."

Ann said, "I was at a crossroad. I could be bitter because
God gave us a Down syndrome child, or I could be open

and be taught. When Sam was two weeks old, I asked God to change my heart so that I could accept my son. I also asked God to forgive me because I prayed he'd take Samuel to heaven."

Each family member traveled different paths of acceptance.

"It took a long time—years—for Marv to totally accept and love Sam for who he is. Who and what helped? God and his love—and Sam himself. It was Sam's love for others and his own sweet personality that won Marv's heart."

Their fourteen-year-old son Colin struggled with resentment for a few months. Reestablishing his relationship with God led to acceptance of his baby brother. During his high school and college years, Colin worked with mentally handicapped men.

Their then eleven-year-old daughter Cameron loved Samuel immediately. Before he was born, she dreamed she was swinging a little blonde boy. Although she could only see him from the back, Cameron told her mother that he was radiant.

Miriam was only three when Samuel was born. When she was five years old, she told her mother, "Mom, I don't want you and Dad to worry. I will always take care of Samuel."

After Samuel's birth, Marv went to the library and read medical journals to learn about Down syndrome. The information was "dark and depressing," Ann said. Sam was also born with a hole in his heart, which was surgically repaired when he was two years old.

And yet, despite the challenges of raising her son, Ann insisted Sam had a profound effect on his family.

"Sam's heart is so pure. He teaches us about God's character. His love is so pure. He forgives instantly. If he had to get a shot, he gave the nurse or doctor a hug or said 'Thank you' because he knew they were trying to help him."

During elementary school, Sam attended a combination of regular and special education classes, as well as physical and speech therapy. As he got older, Sam attended fewer mainstream classes.

"The older Sam has gotten, the greater the gap between his intellect and his 'normal' peers. His mainstream classes were always those within his capability, such as PE or choir. He's always taken special-education classes to help him with math skills, grammar, and life skills. He always understood phonics, and that was good. But he has moderate needs and cannot be left alone."

As a teenager, Sam and his family served at a local soup kitchen. Sam refused to take a break until everyone had eaten.

"Sam loves to give. He loves to serve. He is a popular kid in school because he doesn't see color. He doesn't see name brands. He doesn't know who is popular or not. He just loves people."

Even so, Ann admitted people do not always react well to Sam, seeming to be annoyed or uncomfortable with him. But she and her husband know he is a precious life.

"When Sam was small, elevators scared him. He would throw himself on the floor. People would give him dirty looks. We would always pick him up and give him hugs and kisses. We wanted them to know that Sam was not a throwaway life."

Sam attended several proms during high school. His parents went along with him and his date, a young girl with special needs. During high school, the varsity boys basketball coach asked him to be the team "Spirit Manager." He sang in the high school choir and enjoys having his buddies over.

Sam graduated from public high school when he was eighteen. Ann believes his life is better than what she first imagined for her unborn son.

"There are no typical teenage issues. His school didn't have a senior class trip, so Marv and I took him to Disneyland. He wanted to see Mickey Mouse and Donald Duck. He chose what rides we went on. There was no grumbling, no griping. Samuel is joyful and pleasant. He sees things in such a fun way and he loves to laugh—and to bring laughter to others."

Ann encourages other mothers of Down syndrome children to lean hard on God and to be open to the beauty of the gift.

"Sam is so sensitive to people. We didn't have to teach him that. He was born that way. God gave us this child. I am honored by God's choice. I am blessed. I am taught."

7

That Was Then, This Is Now

The family. We were a strange little band of characters trudging through life sharing diseases and toothpaste, coveting one another's desserts, hiding shampoo, borrowing money, locking each other out of our rooms, inflicting pain and kissing to heal it in the same instant, loving, laughing, defending, and trying to figure out the common thread that bound us all together.

Erma Bombeck

Christa's arrival felt like a you-have-never-seen-anything-like-this case of identity theft. Who I had been disappeared and was replaced by a woman with a stunned looked on her face and a baby in her arms.

I admit it: I had planned my life out. You know what I mean because you probably make plans and enjoy checking off your

"Life To-Do List" too. My "Before Christa" list looked something like this:

Start "emptying the nest"—while realizing adult children often leave boxes filled with their possessions in their parents' basements.

Enjoy more "couple time" with my husband.

Explore the ministry opportunities opening up, like traveling and teaching workshops.

Get back to my writing.

Be intensely interested in Josh's, Katie Beth's, and Amy's love lives.

Christa's birth tore to shreds all my preconceived ideas of how things would play out. I didn't handle it well. I was angry. I was frustrated. I was dreadfully inconvenienced by Christa.

What I Learned Along the Way

To embrace the God-given gift of Christa, I had to let go of a lot of things. I had to abandon my expectations. I had to stop fighting the sudden change of life direction. I had to be willing to walk with a young child again. If I didn't, I would miss all that was wrapped up in my fourth child.

Remember all those other women who told me Christa would be a blessing? Every one of them was right.

I admit mothering a baby who didn't understand the concept of napping was no fun. Despite my success with her siblings, potty training Christa was a challenge. For months she routinely slammed shut the little plastic potty lid and turned her back on the whole process. There were the days when the last thing I wanted to do was color with my five-year-old daughter. I didn't like to color when *I* was five—and I don't like it any better now.

But so many blessings unfolded in the everyday ups and downs of mothering.

Christa brought childhood wonder back to the Vogt family. Christa had never seen snow before, so we all took time to watch the snow fall. We bought new sleds so we could take turns sliding down the hill in our nearby park. We unpacked the older kids' favorite childhood stories—*Goodnight Moon* and *The Big Hungry Bear* and *Curious George*—so that we could read them to Christa. We sang silly songs and played with a stuffed Elmo. We told fairy tales and pretend stories about Christa and sparkly rainbow unicorns.

When my first three kids were younger, they lived near their cousins. Now we live in Colorado while most of Christa's relatives live on the East Coast. We wanted Christa to know her extended family. So after she was born, we made the commitment to go back to visit them every other Christmas. That way Christa gets to celebrate alternating birthdays and holidays in the company of her cousins and aunts and uncles and grandparents.

Hidden Blessing

Like so many of the mommies-come-lately I interviewed, I treasure the hard-earned maturity that I developed during the past twenty years.

By the time Christa rounded out the Vogt family, I'd sought counseling and dealt with some of my stuff. Some of the personal heartache that overshadowed my earlier mothering years with

Changing Traditions

Some Christmas trees are topped with glittering stars or elaborate angels shimmering with gold and lace. But my family's annual Christmas tree is adorned with a handmade aluminum foil and cardboard star my husband and son made nineteen years ago.

The first few years Rob and I were married, preparing for Christmas was almost an afterthought. The holidays were squeezed in between Rob's medical school exams and traveling to visit family. But after Josh was born, I wanted to develop special memories of Christmas for our family.

"We really need a star for the top of the tree," I told Rob as we wrapped multicolored lights around the tree trunk and unpacked our haphazard assortment of ornaments.

"Josh and I can do that," he volunteered.

But instead of setting off to search store aisles, Rob and Josh retreated to the kitchen. With much whispering and laughter—and ample amounts of glue and foil and glitter—they constructed a star.

After all the decorations were hung on the tree branches, Rob lifted our tow-headed son up high on his shoulders. Josh leaned forward and set the slightly lopsided, silvery star in place. And so began our family tradition.

Each December our holiday decorating culminated with Rob helping Josh place the star on our tree. As our family expanded to include two daughters, the tree overflowed with their handmade ornaments. Their hands eagerly fashioned red and green beaded ornaments and painted glass balls. Their chubby-cheeked toddler faces smiled out from photographs glued to construction paper.

And when the last ornaments were hung, Rob always helped Josh place the star on top of the branches. Even during Josh's teen years, my husband pretended to hoist our growing son up

Josh, Katie Beth, and Amy was healed. Pursuing resolution in my thirties produced a sense of stability and peace in my forties. I felt a freedom and special blessing in loving Christa that I had not experienced with my other children. As I held my caboose baby, I was grateful that I no longer wrestled with the anger and bitterness that sometimes had spilled out onto my first three children. If for no other reason than this, I am thankful I am a mommy-come-lately.

high so he could put the star where it belonged. Josh's smile of childish glee and pride changed to laughter. But the tradition remained.

Then my unexpected pregnancy altered our family. Christa was born on Christmas Eve, creating new traditions for our family. Christmas became a time to celebrate two birthdays—the baby Jesus' and our daughter's.

The year Christa turned four, Rob once again brought the plastic boxes of decorations in from the garage. I sorted them out, separating the kids' decorations so that they could find them easily when it came time to decorate the tree. Josh was living in Denver, so I put his box of ornaments to the side, the silver star on top.

"You know, Mom, I think Christa should put the star on top of the tree now," my daughter Amy said.

Change a nineteen-year tradition? No. But throughout the rest of the day, I mulled over Amy's suggestion. And I realized she was right.

Josh would graduate from college in a few months. Except for summer vacations, he had not lived at home in almost four years. In the future Josh would likely start his own family and his own traditions. He might not even make it home for some holidays. Katie Beth and Amy would leave home too.

Would the Christmas star tradition just fade away as Christa's older siblings transitioned into their own lives?

On Christa's fourth birthday, we gathered in our living room. The tree twinkled with multicolored lights and our beloved eclectic assortment of ornaments.

I gave the tattered star to Josh. Josh passed it to Katie Beth, who handed it to Amy. Amy then presented the star to Christa. And as tradition dictated, Rob bent down and lifted Christa onto his shoulders so she could lean in to the tree and place the star on the top branch.

My eyes shimmered with tears as I watched the ending of one tradition—and the beginning of a new one.

When Christa was a newborn, Amy asked me, "How are you going to raise Christa?"

"Pretty much the same way we raised you and Josh and Katie Beth. Dad and I like how you all turned out," I replied.

"But we'll get to spoil Christa, right?"

"Wrong! If we do that, then when you three leave home, Dad and I will be stuck with a spoiled little girl."

115

A Story of Grace

Joe and Torie McGirr had not one, not two, but three children later in life. Their third child, Grace, was born with Down syndrome.

"We were told there was a chance, but we didn't need to know more. I think this really gets down to accepting what life offers—throws—you, really accepting it versus wanting what you want," Joe said. "The future gets heavy, especially since we don't know how functional Grace will be."

"For the record, my analogy of Grace and Down syndrome is this: I look at Conor and say, 'I don't know if he will go to Pikes Peak Community College or to Harvard. But as we get into grade school and high school, that will become apparent, and we'll see,'" Joe said. "Then I look at Grace and say, 'I don't know if she will be very dependent or very functional. Maybe she'll go to Pikes Peak Community College. But I don't need to know that now. We'll see how she does in grade school.'"

It's fun to have a second chance at parenting—to have some experience behind us as Rob and I nurture Christa. Christa has a more flexible bedtime schedule than her older siblings did, but some of the same "dos and don'ts" apply to her because—joy, oh, joy—they worked for our first three children. We're optimistic that Christa will learn to love others, to love God, and to discover her dreams just like her brother and sisters are.

Mommy Guilt

Sometimes I wrestle with mommy-come-lately guilt. For my first three children I was a *young* mommy. Now I am an *old* mommy. It seems like when I turned forty all the warranties on my body parts expired.

Christa gets the mommy whose thyroid went totally out of whack sometime during pregnancy and delivery. For the first six months after Christa's birth, I woke up and wondered how soon I could go back to bed—an impossible dream with a newborn who didn't nap. One of Christa's first words was "TV" because I often turned on children's programs and spent the day snuggled with her on the couch.

My last pregnancy and delivery "blew out the system," so to speak. Christa gets the mommy who has undergone gynecological surgery—and will be having more of the same. Did you know some people train to become a *pelvic reconstruction* surgeon? I envision a white-coated "Bob the Builder" type brandishing a speculum and a scalpel. *Can we fix it? Yes we can!*

When Christa wants to race with me, she likes to yell, "I'm going to beat you!" I just let her run ahead of me. With my physical complications, she will *always* be faster than me. No running races for this mommy-come-lately.

Within a year of her birth, Christa got the mommy who was diagnosed with an unexplained, moderately severe hearing loss. She calls my hearing aids "earrings," not realizing they indicate her mom is considered disabled. No handicapped parking permit for hearing loss, though.

I realize my pregnancy is not the cause of all these things. It's just lousy timing—for me and for Christa.

Willing to Let Go

When Mary had Justin, she let go of her dream job, her career—and she cried for three months straight afterward.

"I knew that being Justin's mom was a whole new chapter in my life. Everything was going to be new—not one thing would be the same. Most everything I'm doing now, I never thought I'd be doing. When Justin goes to swim lessons, I get in the pool

> *I accepted my late-in-life child as a gift from God—and he has been one of my best gifts. And there is nothing like the reality of a baby for helping my teenagers understand how much work is involved in having a baby.*
>
> Karen W., repeater
> mommy-come-lately at
> thirty-nine

too. We go to T-ball practice and soccer practice because those are things Justin wants to do.

"I had to bloom where I was planted. I had to start new relationships, set new goals, pursue new interests," Mary said. "I was thoroughly enjoying being Justin's mom, but I had to find avenues for me like Bible study and MOPS."

The changes Justin went through as he grew from newborn to toddler felt like very small steps—with lots of waiting in between.

"All of the life stages Justin experienced—sleeping through the night, feeding himself, learning to walk and talk—affected what I could do in my life. It takes so long to make it through each milestone of a young child's life. Sometimes it seemed like it would never happen. Then you wonder how it happened so fast. God just really got hold of me and helped me realize all this was his plan for me."

The Bottom Line

It is normal to wrestle with guilt about being an older mom. Go ahead and acknowledge what you wish you could give your late-in-life child: another sibling, a decade-earlier birthdate, or a younger and more energetic mother. Then face the facts:

you are a mommy-come-lately, and there is no turning back the clock!

Let go of what you had before you gave birth and truly grasp all the joys of being a mom. Don't miss out on new opportunities because you're too busy wanting to return to your yesterdays.

Cameo Appearance: **Marlo**

Repeater mommy-come-lately at thirty-five and again at almost thirty-eight

Husband: **Bryan**

Children: **Bethany, age seven; Joelle, age four; Bria and Jayna, two-year-old twin daughters**

"If I would have had it my way, I would have had kids at age twenty-seven," Marlo said. "But my plans are not always God's plans—and that was certainly the case with the timing of having children. Instead of simply getting pregnant like all my friends were doing, I faced infertility. While they were buying maternity clothes and attending baby showers, I was buying fertility drugs and attending doctor appointments."

Marlo underwent scores of tests, trials, drugs, miscarriages—even major surgery—and experienced failure every time. Her first daughter, Bethany, was born through Intrauterine Insemination (IUI). Then came another miscarriage, and Marlo went back to the infertility clinic to try to conceive a second time.

"I thought it would be easy—another IUI or two and I'd be pregnant again. But I wasn't."

After a year of failed IUIs, she went for in vitro fertilization (IVF). Marlo endured two failed IVF rounds and then got pregnant at thirty-five with her second daughter, Joelle. IVF

119

was "expensive, difficult, painful—but in the end it was worth it," Marlo said.

Once her second daughter was weaned, they went back to the fertility clinic again—and Marlo, at thirty-eight, got pregnant on the first try—with twins.

"I hadn't planned on being a mommy-come-lately, but after so many years of infertility, I'm happy to be a mommy at all. I am happy to be a later-in-life mom."

Cameo Appearance: **Dale**

First-time mommy-come-lately at forty-five

Husband: **Lee**

Daughter: **Sarah, age four and a half**

After five years of marriage, Dale's first husband asked for a divorce. Dale was thirty-three years old. She says, "It was a long healing process—and then I met the love of my life when I was thirty-nine."

She married Lee when she was forty-two and then waited only six months to try to conceive. Dale had two miscarriages before giving birth to her daughter Sarah just before her forty-fifth birthday.

"I was so happy that Lee and I conceived three times in twelve months at my age. The physicians were amazed I was so fertile. I'd never tried to get pregnant before then. So I was actually encouraged by the miscarriages."

Even so, Dale said she avoided having a baby shower because she felt she "didn't have a baby until she took her home from the hospital." She was so busy during her pregnancy—taking classes for an art degree and working full-time—that she was detached emotionally.

"I was extremely happy intellectually, but emotionally I couldn't think about the possibility of a third miscarriage.

I'd waited so long to have a baby, and I couldn't bear the thought of being so close and yet so far."

Dale said her daughter will know she is a "truly wanted" child.

"Sarah is hope realized! At my age, I know that the true blessings in life are people and relationships—not the 'stuff' of life."

Like most mommies-come-lately, Dale has learned to laugh about being an older mom.

"I accept that my three-year-old is already saying, 'Mama, you are an old mama. You have wrinkly hands!' But I am also eternally grateful that I am getting to do what I wanted to do all along—be a mom!"

8

Straddling the Parenting Spectrum

> You need to be careful not to say, "We can't." Instead,
> try to think, "How can we?"
>
> Roxanne, repeater mommy-come-lately at thirty-
> five, thirty-seven, forty-two, and forty-five

Christa redefined our family—and stretched Rob and me across the parenting spectrum. Josh was in college, and Katie Beth and Amy were not far behind him. Our budget included disposable diapers and college tuition. We had to figure out how the new, updated Vogt Team was going to work.

Changing My Pace

I was an expert multitasking mom when Christa was born. I talked on the phone while making dinner or folding laundry. I checked English homework while watching the news. Fam-

One Child, Four Car Seats

Christa has four car seats. Sounds absurd, but it is reality. When there are four licensed drivers in the family, one car seat is not adequate. The story I am about to share is true—and I suppose it is funny, if you're not the one stuck in the garage without a car seat.

One morning I needed to run errands. The problem was, over the weekend we'd switched Christa's car seat to Rob's car—and he had driven off with it. I was stranded. All I could do was abandon my plans for the day and wait until he got back home with the car seat.

That evening I plunked down my debit card for a second car seat.

Then came the morning when we were heading out for Christa's "Moms' Morning Out" program. One car seat was in Rob's car. One car seat was in Katie Beth's car. No car seat in mine.

Desperate, I double-buckled then two-year-old Christa in the middle of the backseat and drove oh-so-cautiously to Wal-Mart to buy car seat number three. And, yes, I felt guilty all the way to the store.

I then decreed that one car seat was to remain in my car at all times. No trading. No borrowing. But to be on the more-than-safe side, I accepted a friend's offer of yet another car seat and put it in Amy's van.

One child. Four car seats. Sounds extreme, I know. But take my advice: if you have more than one licensed driver in your family—and they have even the slightest chance of taking your little one somewhere—get a car seat for *every* car. It sure beats being stranded in your garage.

ily life was fast paced, and it didn't slow down for Christa. She admirably kept up with her high-speed family.

Then Christa decided things needed to change. When she was two years old, she began voicing repeated requests for me to "hold-a" her. It took me a few weeks to realize Christa wasn't being endearing with her demands for my time and attention. She was being explicit. She needed me to slow down.

The morning Christa stomped her Elmo-slippered foot and demanded to be held, she finally got my attention. Christa was tired of being lost in a flurry of "wait-a-minutes." She was weary of being swept along in the whirlwind of her older siblings' lives: Sports events. Music concerts. Awards banquets.

I realized my toddler couldn't continue to keep pace with her teenage siblings. I made myself stop and listen when Christa asked to be held rather than putting her off until my to-do list was completed.

It was challenging to shift gears to meet the emotional needs of my caboose child. Usually a train is propelled by its engine. Sometimes the Vogt family train had to allow the caboose to direct its course. I didn't want the words "Wait a minute" to dominate Christa's childhood memories. I wanted her to remember the times we snuggled, the times we read books, the times we sang "The Itsy Bitsy Spider" and she giggled as I tickled her neck.

My older children continued their customary busy lives. They managed homework and work schedules and fun time with their friends. Sometimes Christa and I were a part of their activities, and sometimes we "sat on the sidelines," so to speak. And yes, Christa still needed to wait while I finished a writing project or ran errands. Life does not always progress at a young child's pace. But I guarded against constantly insisting that she do life at everyone else's pace.

Successful "Straddle Parenting"

I think just about everyone who has ever had a child would agree that parenting is exhausting. But being a mom and dad to such a wide-range of ages requires some extra effort at straddling their different worlds and balancing their variety of needs. Here are a few things I've learned.

125

Be Flexible

Sometimes parenting the Vogt family feels like participating in the Parenting Olympics. And just like any good athlete will tell you, flexibility is the key.

Rob and I know our limits now better than we knew them in our twenties. We've learned to say no and to find new meaning in the word yes. At times we needed to divide and conquer, so Rob attended one school event while I attended another. We adjusted schedules to avoid Christa fidgeting through two hours of a band concert. We arrived an hour after it started—but before Amy's participation—and stood in the back while Christa bounced on our shoulders or danced on the stairs.

When Josh lived two hours away from home, Rob took time to get together with him on a regular basis. Sometimes Christa went with him. Sometimes the three of us went together.

When the weather was too cold, snowy, or rainy, Christa watched her sister's soccer games sitting with me in the heated car. Sometimes Rob and I took turns watching the game while we pushed Christa on the nearby swings or helped her master the metal chain ladder.

Participate in Activities All Ages Can Enjoy

As a family, we've gone to the circus, truly something "children of all ages" can enjoy. And Christa's older sisters enjoyed seeing movies like *Madagascar* and *Finding Nemo*.

Colorado is beautiful—and a great place for walking and hiking, which is also an activity for the whole family. Sometimes we have to take shorter or easier hikes to accommodate Christa's ability.

Suggestions from Another Mom Straddling the Parenting Spectrum

Roxanne knows what it's like to live life all over the parenting spectrum. Her seven kids range in age from a nineteen-year-old to a one-year-old. Here's some practical advice from a veteran mommy-come-lately:

Let older kids—not just parents—take turns carrying the younger child when he can't keep up on a hike.

On a camping trip, take along a portable playpen for a young child so he's safe when mom is busy preparing a meal.

While little ones enjoy the slide at a playground, the older kids can toss a Frisbee or even stretch out on a blanket and play a game of cards. Just don't forget to let the younger sibling toss the Frisbee too. Usually he'll tire of it quickly, and the older kids or parents can go back to their fun.

Visit a museum and enjoy a four-year-old child's impression of modern art. Just plan on going through at a faster pace. It may not be a time of art appreciation—but it is family time.

Start game nights with everyone playing. Allow the younger kids to choose games. Let the older kids serve their younger siblings by playing preschool games—at least for a while. Later in the evening, play games for the older kids and parents. Younger ones can team up with mom and dad or help move the game pieces or hold someone's cards.

We joined the YMCA, knowing the older Vogts could exercise while Christa played in the ChildWatch area. But we also make time to take Christa swimming after we've worked out.

Do Age-Specific Activities

On occasion we've done things just with our older kids. We went to see *The Phantom of the Opera*—not a toddler musical—and left Christa at home with her grandmother. If the older kids want to see a special movie, we put Christa to bed and stay up late to watch the movie together.

The same holds true for doing things with Christa. One of my kitchen cabinets is now devoid of Tupperware. Instead, it

Try to stay young. Be willing to be silly. Have tea parties. Do things with them like pillow fights and sleeping in a tent in the backyard. When you are older, it seems like you don't want to do these things. We'd rather read our book on the park bench and get a chance to rest than swing with our little children. I've always tried to keep up on the latest lingo and fads so I can talk with them on their level.

Kim, repeater mommy-come-lately at thirty-five

overflows with crayons and washable markers and coloring books and Play-Doh. My CD changer is full of children's music. I try to say yes to tea parties and dress up.

The first time I found myself back in a McDonald's play area, I experienced a surreal "How did I get here?" feeling. A trip to the mall now includes a stop at the children's play area—unless I can convince Christa it is just too crowded. I don't walk *by* the park anymore—I walk *to* the park, even if it is only for five minutes of swinging and sliding.

My couch is often covered in blankets and transformed into an indoor tent for Christa. My tub overflows with children's bubble bath and toy horses and fishes and mermaids. As much as I am oh-so-conscious of my age, I need to be just as aware of Christa's age—and let her have fun being six years old.

Let the Older Kids Grow Up

Christa was six months old when Josh graduated from high school. So much happened during that time that I almost felt like I missed his celebration. Katie Beth finished her first year of high school, and Amy finished junior high.

I felt like I was living life on two different levels: going forward and fast with the older kids, and going in reverse and slow with our preschooler. I wanted to find some way to get everyone going in the same direction at the same speed.

Life doesn't work that way. Kids grow up—and having a baby sister doesn't change that.

Josh's life moved forward—and out of the home. We celebrated his independence rather than making him feel guilty for adding stress to the family.

As Katie Beth and Amy went through high school, their lives changed too. Their curfews were later, although not always as late as they wanted them to be. Sometimes my expectation of having a readily available babysitter collided with their plans—and I lost. Going out to the movies with their friends sometimes trumped my plans for dinner out with Rob. So be it.

Don't Expect the Older Kids to Be the Parents

I am Christa's mom—Katie Beth and Amy are not. I took advantage of their help while trying not to take advantage of them. I did a lot of "either-or" bartering. "If you'll rock Christa, then I'll fold the laundry—or you fold the laundry and I'll hold Christa." I tried to offer them choices, although sometimes I just said, "Help!" Maintaining balance between relying on older kids' willing help and forcing them into a parenting role they should not play takes a conscious effort at times.

Sometimes Christa got lost in the busyness of her brother's and sisters' lives. Life with the older kids was fast and furious. Everyone was juggling jobs, school, friends, and fun. Sometimes I looked up at the clock and realized it was 9:30 p.m. and Christa

I wanted to enjoy my babies. I was a more experienced, more relaxed mom this time around. But the truth is, I am a really busy mom. Sometimes my older children have played with their baby brothers while I ran errands. My preteen daughters have played endless games of hide-and-seek or decided to put on funny hats and carry musical instruments to parade for their brothers inside on a rainy day. The older brothers wrestle or build with Legos with the younger boys.

Roxanne, repeater mommy-come-lately at thirty-five, thirty-seven, forty-two, and forty-five

was still running around. She was not even close to being bathed and dressed in pajamas.

"Will somebody please put this child to bed?" I asked with a laugh.

And then someone—usually Rob or I—stopped whatever we were doing and took a more-than-willing Christa to bed. Late. After all, *we* were the parents.

Establishing Relationships between Older Siblings and the Caboose

You can't force an older sibling to have a strong relationship with a much-younger brother or sister. The same is true even if your children are born a year apart from one another. In some ways, family is what the military calls a "mandatory formation"—participation is not optional. But you can't determine what those family relationships will look like.

When I was pregnant with Christa, I talked with a friend who had a much-younger brother.

"We really don't have any relationship now," she said. "There are just too many years between us."

Rob and I tried to encourage Josh, Katie Beth, and Amy to be involved with Christa, and they have all chosen to do so. But in the end it was—and will continue to be—their choice.

Give Positive Reinforcement

Positive feedback is powerful. When Josh took time to read Christa a book, I always tried to say something like, "Isn't it nice to have your big brother read you a story?" Or when Amy or Katie Beth took her for a walk or out for an ice cream cone, I thanked them for loving their sister.

I also told family and friends about how wonderful the older kids were with Christa. I made sure they overheard me too.

Go for a Combo

Katie Beth and Amy liked to go to the local bead gallery and make jewelry—sometimes just for fun, sometimes to match their prom dresses. While I am the craft-challenged one in the family, Katie Beth and Amy excel at it. Christa and I went along, and Christa made her own bracelet, usually with her sisters' help.

When a local pottery shop opened, Christa had as much fun slathering a kitty statue with purple, blue, and black paint as Katie Beth and Amy had painting an intricate design on a teacup or plate.

Show Them the Money

If I asked Amy or Katie Beth to take Christa to the play area at the mall, I provided lunch money for them. Sometimes the girls babysat for free—and sometimes Rob and I paid them for their time and effort, especially if they gave up an activity to take care of Christa. We didn't always pay them as much as we would a "real" babysitter, but as the girls got older and were less available, we paid them the going rate.

The Bottom Line

Parenting children that span a wide age range is challenging—but it can be done. Remember these five tips to successfully straddle the parenting spectrum:

1. Be flexible.
2. Think of activities that the whole family can enjoy.
3. Don't forget to have age-specific fun too.
4. Let your older kids grow up.
5. Don't expect your older kids to be surrogate parents to their younger brother or sister.
6. Be liberal with praise and thanks when your older kids spend time with the caboose kid.

Cameo Appearance: **Michelle**

First-time mommy-come-lately at thirty-six, thirty-eight, and two weeks shy of turning forty-one

Husband: **Rick**

Children: **Bryce, age ten; Colby, age eight; Connor, age five and a half**

Despite multiple health problems, Michelle considers herself "a pretty young forty-five." In addition to having three boys, Michelle and her husband are adopting a little girl from China.

"I wanted another baby. But getting pregnant was not a good idea based on my health," Michelle said.

Michelle said she doesn't remember being labeled Advanced Maternal Age with her first three pregnancies.

"I wasn't called anything during those pregnancies, but now that I'm adopting, I'm called crazy."

The road to motherhood was fraught with peril for Michelle. She married Rick when she was thirty-three years old. At the time she taught children's outdoor education classes.

"Even though I loved working with kids, I was content not having children. An infertility specialist told me that I would never be able to have children naturally. I thought about it and decided I didn't want to go through any treatments for infertility."

Rick, who is a schoolteacher, taught kids most of his life too. Unlike Michelle, he wanted to have a family.

Michelle said, "I got pregnant four months after we got married. That pregnancy ended in a tubal pregnancy. Within the next two years, I developed two more tubal pregnancies. Every year of the first seven years of our marriage, I was pregnant. Rick tells me he has never known me nonhormonal—and now I am dealing with perimenopause."

In her thirties, Michelle also dealt with the added problem of endometriosis that went undiagnosed for several years.

"I finally contacted a friend who had endometriosis, and she sent me a book about it. I had all the symptoms." Although her friend's doctor was not on their insurance's preferred provider list, he agreed to see Michelle.

At the same time she started treatment to halt endometriosis, Michelle and Rick went overseas for six weeks to work in a Romanian orphanage.

"The medication caused me to go through pseudo-menopause while we were in Romania," Michelle recalled.

After going off the medication, Michelle got pregnant a fourth time. Her first child, Bryce, was born when she was thirty-six.

After Bryce, Michelle suffered another miscarriage. Then about six weeks into her next pregnancy, she started bleeding. Her doctor said he did not think the pregnancy was viable and wanted her to have a procedure to clean out her uterus.

"I told him I disagreed. I felt very pregnant. He then asked me to come in after the weekend and take a blood test to check my HCG hormone levels—but to be prepared for the procedure. The blood test showed that the HCG levels were going up appropriately. My doctor apologized, saying, 'I am sorry I told you the pregnancy was not viable. It is.'"

Her second son, Colby, was born when Michelle was thirty-eight.

When Colby was two and half years old, Michelle became pregnant again. As she had during her last pregnancy, she experienced bleeding early in this pregnancy. She also dealt with a lot of swelling in her right leg and foot. Her third son, Connor, was born when Michelle was almost forty-one.

"After Connor's birth, I was done. But right after he was born, my husband asked if we could adopt a little girl. That didn't sit too well with me. I was content with three boys. A friend even told me, 'You are a boy mom.'"

Then, at age forty-five, Michelle experienced the "baby wants" again. Rick insisted she was too old to have another baby and told her to "let it go."

"I had just written a letter of recommendation for a friend who was adopting a little girl from China. I realized what a big sacrifice she was making to adopt. And then I called her social worker. My husband had no idea. I asked the social worker questions—and my heart started to change. I talked to a foster mom, and my heart was drawn to little Chinese girls. I wondered what was going on.

"I learned there is always more love to give. There are no limitations. If you have the love and the room—why not adopt? I am excited to open my heart to one more person in my life. God is going to get me through it. Physically, I have some setbacks. Financially, we don't make a lot of money. We do have love. We want to do this."

Michelle admitted she always considered the cost of adopting to be a major obstacle. Michelle is a stay-at-home mom, and Rick teaches middle school.

"Then a friend told me it all works out. She said, 'Yes, it's $20,000—and it all works out.'"

Rick was thrilled that Michelle wanted to adopt. Their boys had always wanted another baby—and Rick and Michelle did not proceed with the process of adopting until they had "planted a seed in them" about adopting a little girl.

"We have a manila envelope labeled 'Little Baby Sister.' We let the boys know this was going to be costly—that we would have to sacrifice things like going skiing. The boys wanted to give money to help adopt their baby sister, so they emptied their piggy banks. We have $50 in that envelope— $30 from the boys and $20 from a friend. Only $19,950 to go."

Michelle insisted this is her story—and that others need to come to their own decision.

"I lost four children through miscarriage, but I have three boys. Now I am adopting a fourth child. It seems to complete things. I am not the perfect mom. I get grumpy and I get tired. But my kids know I love them."

≡ Cameo Appearance: **Scoti**

Repeater mommy-come-lately at thirty-seven (single parent by divorce when youngest son was nine months old)

Former husband: **Bob**

Children: **Kristoffer, age twenty-four; Kyle, age twenty**

Scoti married her husband Bob when she was twenty-two and he was twenty-three.

"We met at college. After we married, we traveled around the world for three years with a music group," Scoti said.

After touring Scandinavia, Europe, Eastern Bloc countries, Israel, Zimbabwe, and South Africa, they finished college. Afterward, they moved to California, where Bob entered the ministry as a music minister. Scoti worked as an editor at a publishing house while Bob became established in his career.

"His parents were bothered that we weren't having kids," Scoti said. "They even sent us a letter urging us to adopt."

Their first son, Kristoffer, was born just two months before Scoti turned thirty-five. Scoti opted for a home birth with both a nurse-midwife and a physician because she wanted to relax at home rather than lying on a delivery table with her feet up in stirrups.

On their fifteenth wedding anniversary, when Kristoffer was three years old, Scoti discovered that Bob was having an affair. Two weeks later, she found out she was pregnant. Nine months after their second son, Kyle, was born, Bob left.

"I am glad I was older when I had my children. I wouldn't have been able to handle both Bob's affair and raising two boys alone when I was younger," Scoti said. "Even though I was physically exhausted, I was more willing to make sacrifices for my boys. It took all my energy to work and take care of Kristoffer and Kyle. I had opportunities to remarry, but I didn't want to subject the boys to the stress of a blended family. If I had been younger, I am not sure I would have been willing to sacrifice my need for companionship and marriage."

As a single mommy-come-lately, Scoti faced the emotional and financial struggles that many single moms endure.

"It would have been nice if someone could have taken my kids for a few hours—or even a day or two—so I could really relax and have some downtime," she said. "I never had enough money for school clothes and supplies. And I needed friendships with married women with kids the same age as Kristoffer and Kyle so that I could evaluate if my kids were normal."

Without the benefit of child support, Scoti worked two or three jobs. She worked full-time at a Christian ministry and also part-time as a writer/editor. She also got up at 3:30 a.m. to bake muffins and cookies to sell at work. The nickels, dimes, and quarters she earned went for gas, milk, and shoes for the boys.

"I was too busy to spend time with friends. I felt so alone. I had all the issues married women had when it came to raising children—plus I had to earn an income too," Scoti said. "I felt so disconnected. I had no one to talk to about parenting two young boys."

A seventy-year-old co-worker, affectionately called "Poppa Gordon," offered to help Kristoffer when he struggled with learning to read. When Scoti's work moved out of state, Poppa Gordon helped her move—even cleaning the carpets in her apartment at 2:00 a.m. after the truck was packed. Poppa Gordon's children considered Scoti and her boys to be a blessing to their father. When his children visited him, they included Scoti, Kristoffer, and Kyle in their family time.

A godly role model, this father of four, grandfather of eleven and great-grandfather substituted as a daddy-come-lately for the boys. When then fourteen-year-old Kyle went to live with his father, he asked, "If Poppa Gordon dies, can I come back for the funeral? Because he was really my dad."

The boys' father died when Kyle was a junior in high school. When Kyle graduated from high school, eighty-eight-year-old Poppa Gordon traveled with Scoti across the country to attend his graduation. Poppa Gordon wanted Kyle to have a "dad" present.

Looking back, Scoti saw one clear advantage to being a single mommy-come-lately: "I had the freedom to instill my moral values in my two boys. I was able to discipline them as I felt was right without arguing with their father about what to do or how to do it."

9

The Other Side of the Story

> I wouldn't be who I am today if I hadn't been born a
> late-in-life child. My family wouldn't be who they are.
> I changed the whole climate of our home in such a
> dramatic way.
>
> Jamie, caboose kid born when her
> parents were both forty-two years old

W hat took you so long to have me, Mom?"
I'm afraid one day Christa will ask me that loaded
question. I try to imagine Christa's perspective on being the
unexpected fourth child in the family. How does she feel about
being a six-year-old child in a family of adults?

Other times I get startling glimpses into my youngest child's
thoughts—and I'm astounded at how perceptive she is about
what is going on.

For example, eavesdrop on a recent conversation between Christa and her then nineteen-year-old sister, Katie Beth. (Christa talks about Maryland because it is where all her cousins live—and where we celebrate her birthday every other year.)

CHRISTA: Katie, when you get married, are you gonna move to Maryland?

KATIE BETH (KB): I really want to stay here, but I don't know. I might have to move if my husband lives somewhere else.

CHRISTA: When you get married you aren't gonna live with us anymore. How will we know where you live?

KB: I'll give you my address and directions to my house so you can come visit.

CHRISTA: When you leave, can I call you if I miss you like I miss Josh?

KB: Absolutely!

CHRISTA: But how will I know what phone number to call?

KB: I'll give you my new phone number, okay?

CHRISTA: Okay. But when you get married, what happens if you forget about me?

KB: I will *never* forget you. You know why?

CHRISTA: Why?

KB: Because I love you, that's why. And if you ever think I'm forgetting or ignoring you, just tell me and I will take you out for ice cream or a movie. You know, though, I'm not getting married for a while. I have to have a boyfriend first.

CHRISTA: Yeah. But what is your boyfriend's name gonna be?

KB: I don't know. And I might not marry my first boyfriend. [*At this point Katie Beth was starting to worry that Christa*

140

was going to ask the first guy she brought home when he and Katie Beth would get married. So she clarified this point with her.] But I don't know what my husband's name is going to be.

CHRISTA: Well, let's pretend your boyfriend's name is Jason and he's in the car with us right now. I'll ask him some questions.

KB: Not right now, hon. [*Katie Beth changed topics because she felt like Christa was thinking too hard about Katie Beth's future.*]

CHRISTA: Okay. But when you do get a boyfriend, you need to call the home phone number and if no one answers, you leave a message on voice mail and say, "Christa, I have a boyfriend and his name is . . ." And then you will have to let me and Mommy and Daddy meet him. And Katie, after you are married, will you still come to my birthdays out in Maryland?

KB: Sure! I'll try!

CHRISTA: So you will just have to tell your husband, "Um

Some of my girlfriends say that they wouldn't have kids in their late thirties or forties because they would be too old to enjoy their children. That is absolutely not the case. My mom is enjoying every minute we have together. Some people think an older mom would have antiquated ideals and not be able to adapt to the culture their child is growing up in. My mom "gets" me better than any of my friends.

Katie, twenty-five-year-old caboose kid

. . . I have to go to my little sis's birthday, but I'll be back in a few days."

KB: But can I bring my husband to your birthdays in Maryland?

CHRISTA: Sure!

When Katie Beth related this conversation, I didn't know whether to laugh or to cry. I did both. I laughed at Christa's wanting to quiz her sister's future boyfriend. And I cried because Christa thought her sister would forget her.

Trying to navigate through life as a mommy-come-lately also means I'm trying to help Christa find her place in our family—and to feel secure in it.

Someone in the Know

In some ways, my friend Jamie understands Christa better than I ever will. Jamie's parents were both forty when she was born. Jamie is now forty-nine and the mother of two children. Like Christa, Jamie has a brother and two sisters who are all much older than she is. Her perspective helps me to understand what special needs my caboose child has and how to meet them. See if her wisdom speaks to you in the following sections.

Sense of Security

When Jamie was born, her brother was fifteen. Her two older sisters were then fourteen and eleven. Each of her siblings played a unique role in her life.

"I had a sense of being special because I had unconditional

love and affirmation from my siblings as well as from my parents," Jamie said.

Her brother Jay, the oldest, was excited about Jamie's birth. His grandmother came to help with the new baby, and he kept asking when she was going home. He wanted to hold his new little sister. For the first two years, Jamie slept in her crib in her brother's room. Jay was "the big brother who fixed things that were broken," Jamie said. "He also watched television with me."

Her sister Jeri read to her and acted out stories with her, while Julie was silly with her. "We'd get in trouble together," as Jamie put it.

Her parents benefited from the older siblings being involved with Jamie. She says, "I think my parents had more autonomy to be who they were without feeling like they always had to be attending to me."

A Letter from Jamie's Mom

Within in a few weeks of finding out I was pregnant, I received this letter from Jamie's mom:

My precious Jamie called to say she had exciting news. "You can't believe what is happening to the Vogts!"

Of course I could—you are going to have a "Jamie"!

I know how mixed your feelings must be . . . just when you have your family life headed in such good directions, you are extending yourself more and more—you and Rob are sometimes able to be a couple again.

And NOW!

Life has taken over your body and soul again!

Looking at our family from this side of Jamie's birth, I am so humbled God took charge of my body to bring such joy and happiness. To see our teenagers develop in such tender ways. None of them felt any neglect or jealousy . . . they really thought I had [Jamie] to make them happy.

Whoever this precious gift may be, I know you will soon be able to treasure each moment.

Even at a young age, Jamie noticed that her parents were more even-keeled and mature than her friends' parents. "The younger parents overreacted a lot," she said. "My parents had been through this. They had fifteen years' experience. They knew what they were doing. Even as a young child I knew that was good. It gave me a very wonderful sense of security."

Independence and Creativity

"Because my siblings were so much older, I developed a lot of independence," Jamie said. "I had to learn to do things quickly to keep up with them."

During Jamie's preschool years, her siblings graduated from high school and moved away to college. She no longer saw her siblings on a day-to-day basis. As a result, "I developed a strong sense of creativity. I had the ability to play by myself and I even had an imaginary friend," Jamie recalled. "It's kind of a nice balance. Like an only child often does, I learned creativity and independence. But I also got the nurturing of multiple relationships, unlike an only child. It was the best of both worlds in some ways."

Sense of Abandonment

Having her siblings leave home—leave *her*—was a struggle for Jamie.

Looking back, Jamie recognized that her siblings' graduations from high school and departure to college were a triumph for them and for her parents. Her reaction at the time was different.

"I didn't think it was a good deal that these people who loved me moved far, far away—and didn't come back very often. It created a significant abandonment issue for me," she said. "And

Easing the Transition

Saying good-bye when older siblings go off to college, leave home, or get married is a fact of life for some caboose kids. "For me, growing up meant going away," said Jamie, who is eleven years behind her closest sibling. After looking back on her own experience, she thought of some ways parents could help ease the transition for their caboose kid:

1. Talk about it.

"I think parents need to tell the younger child that it is not their fault that the older sibling is leaving," Jamie said. "Children have an interesting 'magical' way of thinking that they cause things to happen. As an adult, I know that isn't true, but as a child I wondered if I did something to make them grow up and leave."

2. Create some rituals for the caboose child.

Jamie suggested having the older sibling make a scrapbook with the caboose kid. Fill it with photos of special times they've spent together. The older sibling could also send special little gifts or write letters to their sibling. "I got a couple of those," Jamie said. "It was so cool that I got my own letters."

3. Validate what the little one can do.

While older siblings are off conquering college and careers and married life, caboose kids are achieving their own victories. Jamie had a book titled *Someone I Know* by Carol Madden Adorian that talked about a big sister and a little sister. "Yes, there are things the little one can't do, but there are things she can do. It was a wonderful book. You could use it to talk about the differences between older and younger siblings—and validate what the little one can do." (Note: This book has been re-published under the title *I Can! Can You?* You can order a copy at www.Mommy ComeLately.com.)

4. Be aware of the "unspoken competition."

"Anybody an older sibling dates is going to be competition for the caboose child," Jamie said. "They may not warm up to the outsider. If anyone does win the approval of the caboose kid—well, he or she is worth considering!"

then it happened again when they got married. They moved away—and it felt like they loved somebody else more than they loved me. I don't think I understood at three and four years old why that 'secure network' changed all of a sudden. Everybody was happy about it—except me."

Grandparents' Thoughts

The arrival of a late-in-life child affects an entire family, reaching beyond parents and siblings to grandparents.

Christa's Grandparents

My mom flew across country to be with me nine days after Christa was born. My mom had five children—including my twin sister and me—in five and a half years. Then came ten grandchildren, who all call her "Mimi."

"Holding Christa Jean was a special time for me. We bonded immediately," my mom recalled. "As I held Christa, I didn't feel responsible for any other grandchildren. I could relax and just be with her. It was refreshing because I could give her total, focused attention. We were all united in loving that baby."

Geographical distance has not stopped Christa from having a close relationship with her Mimi. They've sung Barbra Streisand duets together. When Christa wanted to know about Mimi's cat, my mom put together a photo album and mailed it to her.

One day Christa commandeered the phone when she heard me talking with my mom, who struggled with intense knee pain. Christa then proceeded to pray, asking God to help Mimi feel better.

Because of Christa's Christmas Eve birthday, my dad christened her with the nickname "'Twas"—as in, "'Twas the night before Christmas . . ." He and his wife, Jane, met Christa when she was five weeks old. They made an extra effort to add a stopover in Colorado when my dad was traveling on business.

Since my dad was a lifelong fan of musicals, I was not surprised that he talked about Christa by first quoting lyrics to a song: "A line in the movie musical *Babes in Toyland* says, 'Once you cross its borders, you can never return again.' That's what happens when you grow up—you can't return to your childhood. But then when you become a parent, you get to go back again through your children—and again through your grandchildren."

For my dad, Christa is an unexpected chance to experience childhood again. She provides him one more opportunity to splurge at Toys

Grandparents—There or Not?

Many caboose children have grandparents for a much briefer span of their life or do not have grandparents at all. Jamie's siblings have memories of their grandparents that Jamie does not have. For Jamie, it was important to find "adopted grand-

146

"R" Us, just like he did for all his other grandchildren.

"Watching Christa trying to understand when I say, 'Your mother is my daughter,' is fun too," my dad said. "She looks at me and I know she wants to say, 'You're crazy. My mom has always been big!'"

Rob's mom, called "Mimaw" by all four of her grandchildren, lives near us. She is Christa's favorite babysitter—even though she is eighty-eight years old.

"I do whatever she wants me to do," Mimaw said. She watches Christa dress up in princess gowns and plastic high heels and tiaras—and doesn't make her clean up her mess. She sits nearby while Christa plays with her toy horses and tells her Mimaw what to say.

Justin's Grandparents

Mary and Doug's experience is bittersweet when it comes to Justin's grandparents.

Doug's father desperately wanted a grandchild. Unbeknownst to Doug, his father bought a big stuffed teddy bear shortly after Doug and Mary got married. He planned on presenting it to his grandson or granddaughter.

Doug's dad died five years before Justin was born. So Doug's mother presented the teddy bear to Justin, whose middle name is his grandfather's name.

"That teddy bear sat around for a long time waiting for someone to come home," Doug said.

While Doug's mom lives close by, her interaction with Justin is limited because of poor health.

Mary's mom, who is eighty-four, loves being Justin's babysitter.

"Believe me, I watch him like a hawk," she said. "He is very precious cargo."

She often goes on outings with Mary and Justin, visiting museums and parks and riding trains.

"We always bake Christmas cutout cookies," she said. "Justin is getting pretty good at decorating them."

Justin and his grandmother take lots of walks through her neighborhood. Justin always says "Hi" to everyone he meets, telling them his name and then introducing his "Grandma Wells."

"I feel so blessed to have lived so long—almost eighty-five years. Justin certainly livened up this ol' gal's life. I love him very much. He's been my pride and joy."

parents"—or as Jamie says, "little old ladies or little old men who thought I was special and let me call them Grandma or Grandpa."

During high school, one of her boyfriend's grandparents "adopted" Jamie.

Never Underestimate the Importance of Birthday Cards

When Jamie turned thirty-nine, her brother, who was then fifty-four, sent her a birthday card that she vows she will keep forever. It reads:

To My Sister
Celebrating You on Your Birthday

I celebrate you today
I respect and admire you
And the many gifts you share with the world
(INSIDE):
The way you live your life is inspiring to me

And to those who are fortunate enough
To have your special touch in their lives

The letter he included in the card contained the following lines:

"I can count on one hand the number of people I admire for their ability to achieve at their highest potential at every level. And the first one I would mention is my special sister, Jamie. Your life and the way you live it always, yes always, brings tears to my eyes. Congratulations and thank you."

"They wrote me 'grandparent' letters. They even wrote me poems. They sent me a silver dollar on my birthday—even though I was sixteen. I still have those letters. I still have that silver dollar."

Being Little

While Jamie didn't have a competitive relationship with her older siblings, a part of her was trying to catch up to them and to live up to them.

"It took me until I was thirty-five years old to figure out I wasn't little anymore," Jamie said. "Being a size four petite didn't help.

"I compensated by being intellectually intimidating to people my own age. People are really surprised that I feel little or of small consequence. I don't think my siblings acknowledged that I was grown up until I started medical school."

148

In some ways, Jamie felt she had to pass her older siblings' level of accomplishment to earn their respect. She said, "Medical school created a different level of respect. They started asking my advice. I guess it was a signal that I wasn't less than or smaller than they were."

Jamie recommends that caboose children communicate their own milestones to their older siblings. Doing so helps the older siblings realize that "the baby" is growing up.

"I remember being nineteen. I was dating my future husband Marty. He was very tall, and back then he had a full mustache and a beard. We had our photograph taken, and I sent one to each of my siblings for Christmas. That must have been a bit of a shock—their little sister being old enough to date a bearded man."

Other Late-in-Life Children Speak Up

Just like every mommy-come-lately, every late-in-life child has his or her own story. Let's hear from a few more of them.

> *I hate to admit it, but for a long time I was jealous of my older brothers. I realized they would have more time on this earth with our mom. She had the opportunity to see them get married, be there for the birth of their children—and they got a mom in her prime. But I now believe I have the best of her. I am still single with no kids—and I get my mom all to myself. And if you've met my mom, you know this is her prime!*
>
> Katie, twenty-five-year-old caboose kid

149

Emily, Fourteen-Year-Old Caboose Kid

You've heard from Karen (chapter 2) and you've heard from her oldest daughter Beth. Now it's time for Emily, the caboose kid of the family, to give her side of the story.

"I think late-in-life children like me should feel lucky. They are exposed to things that younger parents may not even know happened," she said, explaining that thanks to her parents, she listens to Bob Dylan's music. "Sure, my friends' parents are twenty years younger than my parents, but I like being different that way. It's often interesting to get into those 'Your mom is how old?' conversations. Besides, I'm probably the only one in my class with a mother who remembers wearing a Kennedy button in the 1960 presidential campaign."

Her life is different from her friends' lives in other ways too.

"I've gone through things my friends haven't—like going to my sister's college graduation when I was five years old and being in my sister's wedding when I was eight," Emily said, adding that Beth getting married was tough. "I hadn't realized she'd still be my sister when she got married. I also think there was some 'I don't want to share my sister with anyone' attitude. I'm okay with it now. It kind of grew on me."

Emily laughed about having "weird brother-in-law stories" instead of weird little brother stories.

There was the time Eric let Emily and two of her friends draw all over one of his T-shirts—while he was wearing it.

"That was back when every little girl—including me—had three hundred gel pens. Eric put one of his old T-shirts on inside out and let us color on the shirt—and on him. I think he had about twenty different games of 'Hangman' covering him."

Emily admitted she often feels like an only child, especially when her friends talk about sibling problems, but she added,

"I'm okay with that. I only have to compete with my mom for computer time."

Debbie, Forty-Seven-Year-Old Caboose Kid

Debbie was born when her parents were forty-two. At that time, her siblings were seventeen, thirteen, and eleven years old. As a teenager, Debbie concluded she was a "change-of-life" baby.

"This seemed the logical reason to me why anyone would start all over with diapers and formula when their youngest was eleven years old," she said.

When Debbie was in her twenties, she asked her mom why she was born at such a late time in her parents' lives.

"Mom told me that both she and Dad had lost their fathers the year before I was born. My dad asked her if she would like another child—and she said yes! She said I kept them young."

Debbie's oldest sibling, Ginny, graduated from high school the month Debbie was born. Ginny married when Debbie was four.

"I can't remember life without my brother-in-law, Tom. He is like a blood brother," Debbie said.

Her teen years were difficult because she realized how much older her parents were than her friends' parents.

"I felt like my parents didn't keep up with the times," she said. "My friends' parents seemed more involved with their kids' lives. Mine seemed out of touch."

Debbie wished her parents made more of an effort to get to know her friends and to ask about her life, both in and out of school. She remembers that her sister Bonnie—not her parents— helped her make a decision about which college to attend.

"Looking back, I would have liked my parents to be more involved in my school activities. They never attended any of my sporting events," she said. "Mom and Dad did attend my music performances. But I was terribly hurt when, during my senior year, my mom chose to stay home and watch something on TV. She said the performances were all the same and she didn't want to miss the special on that night.

"I was left feeling they had done all the 'kid stuff' with my siblings. I was just there—alone and isolated," Debbie said.

Matthew, Nineteen-Year-Old "First and Only" Late-in-Life Child

Matt experiences life with the double whammy of being an only child *and* a late-in-life child. His parents tried to have a child for seventeen years, and he was conceived "right at the end of the clock."

When asked about being an only child of older parents, Matt said, "Well, it's like asking me what it's like to breathe. I've never known anything different." He recognizes that because he was an only child, his parents could focus more of their time and energy on him—and he never had to worry who was their favorite child.

"I guess the only disadvantage is that an only child doesn't have as much experience relating to and living with other people—and it can get a bit lonely at times."

Like many late-in-life children, Matt recognizes his parents' maturity. "They have a lot more wisdom than a lot of other parents do because they've lived longer. They've also seen shining examples of how *not* to raise kids."

Matt also acknowledges seeing a more extended generation gap between him and his parents. "We have very different tastes in music. And I love my parents—but they are 'dinosaurs' when it comes to technology. It can be a real pain when your parents have to call you so you can tell them how to turn the TV on."

When Matt considers what his parents have done right in raising him, he becomes effusive.

"My parents have done almost everything right," Matt said, adding that he would be amazed if he was able to match his parents' love and care. "My parents have not ceased to pray for me, my friends, my future wife, and their future grandchildren since they found out they were going to be parents."

The Bottom Line

Late-in-life children are just that—children—but they are often living life with much older family members: parents, siblings, and grandparents.

Help your child feel more secure by discussing all the changes going on around her.

Deal with your child's issues and questions in an age-appropriate manner, but don't avoid the real issues of life that affect late-in-life children.

Ask your child how she feels about changes related to older family members: her brother going to college, her sister getting married, or her grandfather's death.

Cameo Appearance: **Jeanne**

Mommy-come-lately at thirty-five and again at thirty-seven

Husband: **Wendel**

Children: **Caleb, age three; Connor, age twenty-one months**

Jeanne believed God had promised her a child, but she did not know how he would fulfill his promise. After years of unsuccessfully trying to get pregnant, Jeanne and her husband Wendel decided to build their family by adopting.

"When a birth mom asked us if we would adopt her child, we realized this was the answer to our prayer," she said.

Three months later, they adopted their son Caleb. Then, seventeen months later, they completed another round of paperwork to adopt. They waited three months before they received the call that they were once again selected to be adoptive parents. A mere ten days later they brought home their second son, Connor.

"Having experienced infertility, I have such joy in finally being able to put on the 'mommy' hat. The wait made me appreciate our children so much more!"

Even so, becoming a stay-at-home mom was an adjustment for Jeanne.

"I love being at home with my boys, but I had so much time to be my own person before children. It has been an adjustment to be continually content with the role in which I now find myself," she said. "I am not able to be involved with activities outside the home right now. But I know this is only for a season, and this season will pass quickly. I've had to let go of some expectations because time is now consumed with two little boys and dishes, diapers, and laundry."

Jeanne loves being a late-in-life mom, saying her two sons have brought her joy, amazement, and wonder.

"I take more time to sit on the carpet and build block towers with them. I watch my sons' concentration in getting that next block on the tower—as well as watch them develop other skills. I have grown so much as a person by being a late-in-life mom. I am thankful some of my self-centeredness is being replaced with selflessness."

During the years she faced infertility, Jeanne said, she realized she was not in control of her life.

"I went from thinking I could control pretty much everything to realizing that God controls my life—and that he gives me the opportunities to relinquish what I thought I controlled to him."

Jeanne said her faith in God deepened as she waited for a child. When she was discouraged, she remembered that God had a perfect plan for her life.

"I had to come to the point where I was willing to completely give up my desire to be a mother into God's caring hands. I learned to speak my deepest heart to God—and to wait to hear his response. When I shared my hope of being a mom with him, he gave me the promise that he would give me a child," Jeanne said. "He does not often speak to me in that way, but it gave me hope and something to hold onto when my friends all had babies and my arms were still empty."

Cameo Appearance: **Peggy**

Repeater mommy-come-lately at thirty-six and again at forty

Husband: **Jim**

Children: **Jeff, age forty-two; Jim, age forty; Jay, age twenty-nine; Katie, age twenty-five**

Peggy and her first husband divorced after ten years of marriage. She was a single mom of two young boys when she met her second husband, Jim. After putting herself through nursing school, Peggy met Jim when he began his first year of residency.

Jim's family resisted their marriage. Peggy was seven years older than Jim, was divorced, and was also "just a nurse."

"His father couldn't figure out why his well-educated, handsome son wanted to marry a 'used' woman," Peggy said.

"He said there were plenty of single, young women doctors or nurses Jim could marry."

Peggy's future sister-in-law told her that she could sway her father to approve the marriage if Peggy agreed to certain conditions. She then told Peggy that if she got pregnant, she needed to agree to have an amniocentesis. If something was shown to be wrong with the baby, Peggy needed to agree to have an abortion.

"I was told they didn't want any retardation in their family tree. I wasn't a Christian at that time, and it sounded reasonable to me, so I said okay."

Peggy got pregnant quickly and, as agreed, went to Johns Hopkins to have an ultrasound. She recalled watching the monitor and seeing her seventeen-week-old baby moving away from the ultrasound. She had to wait two weeks for the test results.

But Peggy's faith had grown since she had married Jim.

"I was raised by devout Christian parents, but even so, I just didn't understand what it all meant. I searched for peace and happiness in my heart and soul for so many years. I thought it was the lack of something—having a child, becoming a nurse, getting remarried."

During this time, Peggy felt overwhelmed by marital struggles. She was so discouraged she sat in her car and sobbed.

"I remember my mother saying to me, years before, 'When you get tired of trying to run your life, if you will give it to Jesus, he will make it right,'" Peggy said. "I prayed out loud to God, telling him I was willing to let him take my life. I had chased so many rainbows thinking it would bring me happiness and peace. Nothing worked. I admitted to making a huge mess of my life. So, being brash and ignorant, I even gave God a timeline. Can you believe that? I told him I would try it for a month. He could have my life, and I'd see if my mother was right."

Later that same day, Peggy went grocery shopping. The young man checking her groceries talked with her about God and invited her to his church. She began attending with her two young boys. Jim eventually came to church too because he wanted to know what had changed her.

As a new believer, she realized that no matter what the test revealed, the baby was a gift from God.

"I prayed the baby wouldn't have Down syndrome, but I also didn't care. I believed the Lord would provide for us no matter what."

After their son Jay was born, Peggy and Jim talked about trying for more children. But when she did get pregnant again, she miscarried at twelve weeks. And as months passed, she still didn't get pregnant again.

"I couldn't understand it. We tried and tried—and I didn't get pregnant. I thought it wasn't meant to be."

Then, at thirty-nine, Peggy began dealing with severe heartburn and chest pain. She went through a series of medical tests. Because gynecological problems developed, her doctor recommended a hysterectomy.

"The morning of the surgery I felt sad. Then the doctor came in and told me I was pregnant!" Her surgery was canceled, and Peggy began preparing for her fourth child.

"There seemed to be this stigma: you're too old to be having a baby. People look at you funny," Peggy said.

This time, she said no to amniocentesis.

"I wasn't going to abort this baby, so there was no sense in doing it."

Peggy's family was not supportive of her pregnancy. When she asked her father why he didn't seem excited, he said, "Because I don't want you to keep doing this." Her brother, who has a mentally handicapped child, wrote her a long letter urging her to "get rid of" her baby. He said she didn't know the sorrow of raising a mentally handicapped child.

"Even so, I had a peace about the baby. I told God that he could give me whatever he wanted to give me."

When she was forty, her daughter Katie was born. As Katie grew up, Peggy was aware of the age gap between her and the moms of Katie's friends. When Katie started preschool at age four, Peggy worried about how much older she was than the other children's moms.

"I felt so bad because I could be the mother of those younger moms. But Jim told me kids don't notice age."

A few weeks later, Peggy finished up Katie's bedtime ritual of reading books, singing a song, and saying prayers. As Peggy walked out of the room, her daughter called her back.

"Every night you put me to bed and sing and say prayers," Katie said. "And I look up at you and I think how really old you are. And then in the morning I am amazed and surprised you are still alive!"

Peggy didn't know what surprised her more: that her daughter thought she was really old—or that she used the words "amazed and surprised."

As a mommy-come-lately, Peggy felt she better understood what her children needed.

"I realized with my two late-in-life children that they needed to be connected with things like soccer and Little League and drama. I wasn't trying to finish nursing school. I had no other agenda. That changed my parenting of Katie and Jay.

"When I was twenty-five and thirty, I was so wrapped up in me. Parenting was a job. Now it is a pleasure. Late-in-life children really are a blessing in disguise. The critics speak in ignorance. Every baby is a gift from God.

"I never thought about time when I was young. Now I think about time and how it impacts my children. If I live to be as old as my parents, I have only ten or fifteen years left with Katie."

10

Embracing My Mommy-Come-Lately Life

Emily has opened new worlds to me. Because of her, I know the words from Broadway musicals I never heard of. I can find every high school in the area that puts on musicals. I can recognize a good audition song. I know where the books on forensic anthropology are in the library. I can tune a snare drum. When I was fifty years old, I learned to swim so Emily wouldn't be in the deep end of the YMCA pool alone.

Karen, repeater mommy-come-lately at forty-two

What was I doing at a MOPS (Mothers of Preschoolers) meeting?

Somehow I missed out on MOPS during the years my first three children learned to sleep through the night, use the potty, and recognize colors and numbers. My support was an informal group of other young mothers. We traded babysitting, pushed strollers to the park, and empathized with one another over the phone about discipline and ear infections—all the while fending off repeated demands for juice and Cheerios.

Years later, I stood among women gathered in small groups, their voices an inviting blend of laughter and friendly chatter. Some had tummies protruding beneath maternity tops. Others held young babies in their arms. Most were in their twenties or early thirties.

And there I was: forty-four years old, the mother of a then twenty-year-old son, seventeen- and fifteen-year-old daughters— and my then two-year-old unexpected blessing, Christa.

Most of my friends have older kids. We survived toddlers, conquered preadolescence, and wended our way through adolescence. We don't talk about diaper rash. Instead we debate curfews, dating, and college choices. Requests for McDonald's Happy Meals have been replaced with requests for the car keys.

Toddlers were long, long ago . . . until Christa arrived on Christmas Eve 2000.

When I told an acquaintance about my unexpected pregnancy, I watched as her eyes filled up with tears. She hugged me and expressed her excitement.

"It will be interesting to see how God keeps you connected with younger women," she commented.

Never did I imagine she meant I'd attend MOPS. Being there felt uncomfortable—kind of like trying on my high school pompom uniform again. Sure, it fit twenty-eight years ago. But now I would look ridiculous in the short maroon pleated skirt and oversized white sweater emblazoned with a *B*.

That's how I felt standing in the midst of all those young moms: ridiculous. Mothering preschoolers—been there, done that. I am a mother of a preschooler *again*.

However, Christa's arrival directed me to MOPS. I read information in the church bulletin but told myself I didn't belong. Those women were focusing on motherhood for the first time; I was going around the block again. Since my first three attempts at mothering didn't fail, surely I could succeed with Christa.

Despite my resistance, the thought "Just try one meeting" echoed through my brain. With much hesitation—and a lot of internal kicking and screaming—I attended my first MOPS meeting. What would it hurt, besides my pride, to sit among unwrinkled, twentysomething moms?

I was trying to remember what mothering a preschooler was like. Potty training Christa seemed daunting, even while I reminded myself that my older children mastered it. Would I remember how to lovingly discipline a three-year-old? Would I be able to give Christa the time, attention, and energy she needed?

As I sat down with my newly assigned small group, I feared only two things: telling these young women my age and trying to survive making crafts. You would think that I was going to have to perform brain surgery. It's a good thing I didn't know about the craft requirement *before* the meeting.

Ruth, the group leader, welcomed us and started off by telling us a bit about herself. She then turned to me. I took a deep breath and began talking.

"Hi, my name is Beth. My husband and I have been married twenty-three years." Their eyes widened.

"I have a twenty-year-old son, Josh."

Now I heard their mental calculators clicking as they tried to figure out just how old I was. At the same time, it dawned on me: I could be the mother of some of these girls! Quickly, I mentioned my two teenage daughters and, finally, my toddler.

Our getting-to-know-you chatting ran over into the craft time. We all voted to meet within the next few days for coffee and crafts. What a relief! I prayed I'd come down with the flu or something before having to handle a glue gun.

Within weeks of my first meeting, I became quite the hot commodity among the other moms because *I had two daughters who babysat*. When someone asked for my phone number, I wasn't sure if they wanted to talk to me—or call Katie Beth or Amy to set up a babysitting time.

During my time in MOPS, I learned to quell the thought, *Oh, you seem like such a nice young girl. I should introduce you to Josh.* I'd remind myself that the "nice young girl" was married and the mother of a preschooler!

Getting involved with these moms of preschoolers reminded me how I valued friendships with other moms during my first go-round at raising children. One of my greatest joys of mothering is the relationships I developed with other mothers. MOPS provided an opportunity for coffee, conversation—and yes, even crafts. During each meeting I saw women laughing together, hugging one another, and comforting one another when their morning routines went haywire. What mother—be she twenty or forty—doesn't want a friend or two to walk alongside her during the toddler years? Sure, I had been around the block a few times. As I went around again, did I want to go it alone? No. Besides, I'd answered some of the questions young mothers pondered about being a mom. Maybe I could share a solution or two along the way—and learn some new things too!

Feeling at Home

Just as we did on our way to motherhood, Mary and I took divergent paths and arrived at the same place: MOPS. I went with much hesitation—and Mary pursued MOPS with much persistence.

"I ran as fast as I could to MOPS—and then I couldn't get in because there was a waiting list," Mary recalled. "Justin was a year old. I had questions. I needed relationships badly.

"When I first called, I told the lady I talked to that I was forty-six years old. She said, 'There won't be anybody in your age group, but that's okay. We'd love to have you, but there is a waiting list.'"

Mary called every two weeks for two months before getting in to the group.

"I think the coordinator wanted me to stop calling her," Mary said with a laugh. "I think they made a space for me."

The women in Mary's MOPS group treated her like gold, Mary said. "They were friendly—asking about me and what I was interested in. They were very inclusive. I felt like I was one of them. I felt like I was home."

She struggled to explain how much she valued MOPS. "Everything we did was fun, and I made a lot of friends. I remember walking out of MOPS one day. I had my little craft and Justin had his little craft. And I remember thinking, 'This is awesome, so meaningful.' We had both experienced relationships, and we had made a craft, and our needs were met. I remember how happy he was and how happy I was."

Mary still has close friendships with two of the women from her original MOPS group.

"These other moms walked the path ahead of me. Whenever I had questions, they would say, 'This is what you need to do.'"

Mary shed a few tears remembering how precious those years with MOPS were.

"It is a spiritual milestone I will never forget. God answered my prayers for relationships with other moms. I was stabilized. I knew how to take care of myself as a mom and as a woman."

Living in the Now

My life looks nothing like it did six years ago.

Rob retired from the Air Force and opened a solo family practice office, which is akin to jumping out of an airplane and waiting for your parachute to open.

Josh graduated from college, got his first job, pursued his writing career, and got married!

Katie Beth entered nursing school, which meant I had to get used to the idea of my daughter working with cadavers in anatomy lab.

And Amy graduated from high school, spent a summer in Guatemala, and started college.

To a great degree, all of those experiences fell into what I expected my life to look like in my forties. With Christa, the terrain of motherhood is familiar — but hardly identical to parenting my first three children.

I no longer have the luxury of sleeping late, because Christa's morning routine includes her sneaking out of her bed and into ours. She likes "cimmamom toast" and sparkling cider or milk for breakfast.

Too often the TV is turned on to the Disney Channel or Nick-elodeon. I tell myself it isn't an unforgivable parental mistake. Every morning Christa fusses over wearing tights or socks. She sits in her special chair while I reteach myself how to fashion a French braid or some other girly hairstyle involving barrettes and rubber bands.

I write when Christa is at kindergarten. I have a few precious hours when I don't struggle between getting done what I want to get done and my six-year-old saying, "But Mom, I want to play with you *all the time. What can we do now?*"

I am the mom of four children. But during this season of my life, I feel like I am the mom of an only child. I can't say, "Go play with your brother" or "Stop fighting with your sister" because that isn't an option in Christa's life. Amy does like to tease Christa, insisting this is her only chance to tease someone younger than she is.

When I run errands, I only have one child to buckle into a car seat. Only one child walks with me through the grocery store and pulls cereal boxes or candy off the shelf, chanting, "Buy this! Buy this!"

The spring break before Amy graduated from high school felt more fractured than "family affair." Josh was working at his first real job. Katie Beth flew back East to spend a week with my younger sister—visiting her aunts and uncles and cousins and grandparents. Amy embarked on a road trip to Arizona with five girlfriends. Rob and Christa and I were the homebodies. Rob planned on taking off two days for fun with Christa. The rest of the time, I planned some activities.

Disney Princesses on Ice was in town. So I decided to start the week with a surprise—and bought tickets for Christa and me. In my first life as a mom of three, I bought tickets in the general seating area. But with Christa, I decided to splurge and buy tickets for seats up close to the action.

In the past, our children were warned, "Don't even ask," as we herded them past the $8 snow cones or $10 programs. This time, when Christa was enthralled by the glowing star princess magic wand ($16), I thought, "Why not?" and splurged again.

As much as mothering Christa is like mothering my first three—when to say yes, when to say no, when to push her to try something new, when to let her choose—it is so different.

Being a repeater mommy-come-lately is challenging. The reality is, I am raising two separate families. I try to keep Christa connected with Josh, Katie Beth, and Amy. But just as much as she is their younger sister, she also lives the life of an only child. And I can't change that.

Instead, I try to accent the positive. I expressed appreciation for the time Josh invited all three sisters up to Denver and treated them to dinner and a tour through the Denver Aquarium. I am thankful when Katie Beth and Amy take Christa out for a "girls only" shopping and lunch date. I also learned to deal with the negative—like the times when an overtired Christa breaks down and cries because she misses Josh. I hold her and tell her I miss him too.

I was only partly right all those many years ago when I threw up in the bucket beside my bed and thought my life was over. As much as I tried to keep everything the same, I had to walk away from things I loved. Once Christa was born, teaching workshops and women's Bible studies no longer fit in my life. But even as I closed the door on those activities, I was redirected to a dream I'd put aside while I raised my first three kids: writing.

Somewhere in the midst of our family's expanding from five to six, I thought, *If I wait to write until Christa grows up, it will never happen.*

And so, even as I let go of the life I'd established, I began to explore writing again. Just like Christa took baby steps as she learned to walk, I took baby steps too—completing a correspondence course; attending writers' conferences; joining Inkspired, my writers group; and having articles published.

Christa enjoyed telling people, "My mommy has a book contract!"

One day I asked her, "Do you know what the book is about?"

Silence.

"This book is about you, Christa. If you hadn't been born, I wouldn't be writing this book."

As I discovered each of my children—who they are, what their strengths and weaknesses are—I discovered myself. Watching Christa grow up is like unwrapping an unexpected gift filled with laughter and an unlimited supply of hugs, kisses, and childlike wonder.

> *I didn't live my life under the Advanced Maternal Age label—I didn't even see the label. I just had children. I knew I was older. My body felt old, but my brain never felt old. I don't care what others think.*
>
> Patty, repeater mommy-come-lately at forty-one

At the same time, I rediscovered a bit of my heart that was set aside while I mothered Josh, Katie Beth, and Amy. I had to look past all my plans—to be willing to let God interrupt my life in an unexpected way—before I could embrace my late-in-life child.

When I stopped writing years ago, I thought, "Maybe the next time I sit down to write, I'll have something to say."

I had no idea.

Just in Time

"From the first moment I laid eyes on Justin, I've been doing a double-take. I can't believe this child is really mine. Since having a child never really seemed possible, it's hard to believe he's here. To this day I am thankful I am his mom," Mary said.

But even so, she admits having a child changed *everything*.

She and Doug lived life in reverse and had their empty nest before Justin was born.

"I know it sounds odd, but we had time to travel and play when it was just the two of us for eleven years. We visited relatives across the United States. We purchased property in the mountains, with plans to build a retirement cabin. We still have the property, but Justin and his dad will probably build the cabin now, sometime down the road."

Mary and Doug traveled to Canada, England, Israel, Italy, Germany, and Switzerland. They camped and fished in the backcountry of Alaska and in Wyoming and Colorado. Dinner dates and Broadway shows were frequent—as well as professional sports events. They also worked in their church's children's and youth ministries and volunteered in homeless shelters.

With Justin's birth, their lives took a 180-degree turn *for the best*.

"Most of what we did in our former life has completely changed. We don't do what we used to do because it doesn't fit right now. We plan our vacations with Justin in mind, looking for fun things he can do too, like swimming and tubing and throwing rocks in the water."

Another big change occurred when Mary went from "warp speed" in her communications career to being a stay-at-home mom and now a work-from-home mom.

Marlo's Top 5 Tips for Working Mommies-Come-Lately

1. Put a high priority on tummy-tickling, puzzle-solving, and reading stories to your children. Don't miss the fun stuff.
2. Multitask when you can. Read a book while you're taking a relaxing bubble bath.
3. Cut out the less important stuff.

Maybe you can limit long phone calls or keep your emails short.
4. Be organized. Write lists to keep on track with all your to-dos.
5. Fit your time together like pieces of a puzzle. Include things like rest, leisure activities, and fun outings as pieces of that puzzle.

"I no longer travel the country attending business meetings. As the editor of *MOMSense* magazine, I spend hours at lunch meetings and writers' conferences. I don't shop for the latest business attire—I wear 'mom casual.' I spend more time shopping for clothes for Justin, who seems to be in a continual growth spurt.

"I wouldn't change my new and improved life for anything. Six years ago, if you had told me that I'd have a child, quit my corporate communications job, and work from my home office for MOPS International, I would have told you that was impossible."

After Doug was elected sheriff, Mary slowly got back to work by picking up freelance editing and writing jobs.

"My brain needed to reengage, so I found several contract jobs to keep me fresh in the writing arena. I worked while Justin, who was then two years old, napped or after he went to bed at night," she said, admitting it is hard to switch gears and be creative when she is exhausted from a day in the life of a busy boy. "I named my company Just in Time Communications, because Justin came 'just in time.' Not necessarily my timing—I'd have

There are seasons where the focus of life shifts. That's okay! This is mommy season. But you can keep in your life those things that are important to you. Focus on what is important, organize so you don't miss the good stuff (either with your kids or your activities), and remember that these years are short. You've had more years to gather wisdom and maturity. You're at an advantage in raising kids. Rejoice in that!

Marlo, repeater mommy-come-lately at thirty-five and again at almost thirty-eight

preferred he had been here a little earlier so I'd have more energy—but in God's timing."

Mary contacted MOPS about writing projects too, first editing one of their books and then being selected editor of *MOMSense*.

"Only in God's economy would I be an editor for *MOMSense* magazine at fifty-one. But it works because I am a mother of a preschooler. I work about twenty-five hours a week, juggling my schedule and time with my son and my husband. I work harder as a freelance editor than I ever did in the corporate world."

Mary is not surprised by how active life is with Justin, since he moved constantly in utero. Her biggest struggle since Justin was born is finding the energy to keep up with her "Energizer Bunny" boy.

"I work at staying physically fit, watch what I eat, ride my bike, and take nutritional supplements. I want to be with Justin for the long haul. I would like to see my grandchildren—who he is already making plans for!" Mary said with a laugh.

Life with a young boy is one of continual motion. Mary's day-to-day activities with Justin are a far cry from her twenty-six years in the corporate world.

"We build with Legos, color and paint pictures, read stories, and make greeting cards for our relatives. We play with his elaborate train set, play with dinosaurs and cars and trucks, sing songs, and watch children's DVDs over and over again," she said. "We plant flowers and pick vegetables and look for roly-poly bugs and worms and slugs, and we dig in the sandbox and dirt together. We do all the 'boy' things."

Depending on the season, Justin swims or plays soccer or T-ball. He enjoys going on outings with his grandmother and attends preschool, Sunday school, and Vacation Bible School.

"Ours is a busier than normal lifestyle, but I savor each new experience I have with him because it is so out of the ordinary at my age."

Back when she was pregnant, Mary and Doug listened as a medical technician worried about how one of her kids was doing in school. When Doug asked if parents ever stopped worrying about their kids, she said no. Mary now knows the technician was right.

"I'm concerned about making all the right decisions about school, friends, activities, and his spiritual life," Mary said. "I search and research the best possible *everything* for him. I want to be a good steward of his life—but I know at times I'm too obsessed with making the right choices, so I am trying to give God my worries."

When she was selecting a kindergarten class for Justin, Mary stood in line in the dark at 6:00 a.m. in freezing temperatures to get an application for a recommended kindergarten program. As she began this new adventure, Mary was thankful that her original MOPS coordinator, Kendra, was also now a dear friend. Because

Kendra's kids attended the same school, she helped Mary adjust to Justin's new school and all the changes.

"Justin's life is arranged much differently than most kids', but God has that under control. Aunts, uncles, grandparents, and parents are all older. Even our dog is older. He's fifteen years old and most of the time would rather sleep than play. There aren't any kids Justin's age in our neighborhood. Justin doesn't have any cousins his age. His closest first cousin is thirty-seven.

"When I walk into a group of people, I find myself looking for moms of all ages to talk to because I belong to the 'Mommy Club.' I especially look for late-in-life moms to swap stories and words of encouragement."

The Bottom Line

Just as my life is so different from what it was six years ago, your life changed when you became a mommy-come-lately. Don't fight it. You'll only get worn out.

Don't go it alone. Motherhood is best experienced in the context of relationships with other moms. It is not for the fainthearted, and it is not a life meant to be lived solo.

Be willing to let go of what was. Only then can you embrace life now.

Cameo Appearance: Susie

Repeater mommy-come-lately at thirty-eight

Husband: **Pat**

Children: **Zachary, age thirteen; Alex, age eleven; Piper, almost two**

Susie and I met when we both lived in Florida and attended the same women's Bible study. Pregnant with her second child, Susie was also my husband's OB patient.

When Susie was seven months pregnant, her husband, Mark, an Air Force pilot, was killed in a plane crash. With an unwavering faith in God, Susie became the single mother of two young boys.

I rejoiced as within two years, Susie fell in love and married Pat. Her son Zachary was then four years old, and Alex was almost two years old.

"Pat and I decided that we were very happy with the challenge of two boys. That was quite enough kiddos, thank you!" Susie said. "We were not planning on having any more children."

But, as the poet said, "The best-laid plans . . ."

"I went to the doctor to be sure my home test was not accurate. Much to my surprise, I was, indeed, pregnant!"

Susie found out she was going to be a mommy-come-lately when she overheard a conversation between her doctor and a resident. Sitting in an exam room, Susie heard her physician say, "Oh, this is going to be fun!"

"Immediately I knew they were going to tell me that the little stick was pink."

At thirty-eight, Susie struggled with the challenge of redefining what her life would look like once the baby was born. At that time, her sons were independent nine- and eleven-year-olds.

"I was just getting into the days when I had more freedom—looking toward the possibility of taking on more ministry opportunities during the day while they were in school and having lots of extra time for non-mom endeavors," Susie said. "I struggled with the reality that

I would be back to naptime schedules, lots more time at home, and having a baby strapped to my hip."

As her pregnancy progressed, Susie was excited to feel her baby kick and move.

"I hoped I would be a more relaxed parent this go-round and take more time to really enjoy each stage. The big question was whether I would have the energy to stay on top of everything. Maybe I need to invest in a motorized scooter and a bullwhip," she said with a laugh.

Susie felt catapulted into a higher risk category—and at twenty weeks, an ultrasound detected cysts on her baby's brain that were a possible marker for Down syndrome.

"We were given the option to see a perinatologist for further testing as well as to consult with a geneticist. After much prayer and talking with a family friend who is a physician, we were confident in our decision to have a 3-D ultrasound, but not amniocentesis," Susie said. "The point was made that unless further testing would change our decision to have the baby—which was never an option—or give us more peace, there was no need to have a test that could put our baby at risk."

The ultrasound revealed that the cysts had resolved and that there were no other markers for Down syndrome.

"Even though I think I'm in control of my life, anything can happen. I'm thankful God reminds me daily, 'I know the plans I have for you . . . plans to prosper you and not to harm you, plans to give you hope and a future'" (Jer. 29:11).

Susie wondered how Pat would handle labor and delivery, saying, "Pat does not have the stomach for anything medical. Much to my relief and delight, he was a great coach through labor—although he did stop at McDonald's on the way to the hospital. All the while he was ordering, I was contracting and breathing."

176

Piper, a healthy baby girl, changed the family for the better.

"Life with Piper is so much fun. We call her the 'JFB' — the Joy-Filled Baby. Her brother Zach will often get her when he comes in after school, take her to his room, and just play with her. Her other brother Alex loves to make Piper laugh. He enjoys being the much-older, strong, macho brother. Piper goes in every morning to wake Alex up. She crawls on top of him and playfully slaps him in the face until he wakes up."

Cameo Appearance: **Lisa**

First-time mommy-come-lately at thirty-six

Husband: **Dave**

Daughter: **Rachel, age six**

While mothering her daughter Rachel, Lisa has learned to live with lupus, a chronic illness that caused secondary infertility.

After dating for two years, Lisa and Dave married when she was twenty-nine and he was thirty-six. They were both open to having a child. But since Dave was launching his graphic design business, they decided to wait two years.

During that time, Lisa opened her physical therapy practice. Their two-year plan was still the goal. But Lisa began suffering body pain and headaches and was diagnosed with fibromyalgia. Then Lisa was involved in an automobile accident when another car broadsided her car, further delaying their dream of starting a family.

The accident also wrecked her health, exacerbating her fibromyalgia and triggering lupus. Her symptoms included exhaustion, joint and muscle pain, and severe, sometimes constant migraine headaches.

"I couldn't see the light at the end of the tunnel,"
Lisa said. "I had to get someone to take over my physical
therapy practice. Ultimately, I had to close it. It was a huge
disappointment, but I always hoped to do it again. And I
couldn't get pregnant because of the medications I was
taking."

Lisa battled health problems for three years. She
developed high blood pressure, gained forty pounds, and
developed prediabetes. Finally Lisa tapered off the steroid
medication she'd been taking. She also managed to lose the
extra weight. Since Lisa felt so much better, she and Dave
decided to start their family.

"I got pregnant within the first month. I was thirty-five,
so my chart was stamped 'AMA.' It didn't matter. I was a
young AMA," Lisa said. "My ob-gyn was supportive because
she knew how many children I wanted to have. She told me
being thirty-five was nothing to worry about. Her children
were born when she was forty and forty-two, so she was a
mommy-come-lately too.

"I never thought I'd be older and having children.
Having to wait had been frustrating. Now there was a real
eagerness to make the most of being pregnant. I felt like I
was assisting God in creating a miracle—the miracle of my
child."

Despite her chronic illness, Lisa's pregnancy went well.
During the first months after Rachel was born, Lisa was on
an emotional high.

"I'd been in a quagmire of medical problems before
Rachel," Lisa said. "Now my life was finally moving forward."

However, within a few months, Lisa once again dealt
with physical problems. Because lupus can cause joint and
muscle pain, Lisa had difficulty just holding her newborn
daughter. Then when Rachel was nine months old, Lisa had

jaw surgery. Because she would be under general anesthesia, Lisa had to stop breastfeeding.

Lisa began to realize Rachel might be her only child. She wanted to take care of Rachel all by herself. But by the time Rachel was four years old, Lisa was worn out.

"I didn't ask for help. I had said good-bye to my career and threw myself into mothering. Maybe I embraced it too much. I tried so hard and ended up with no reserves. And since Dave is self-employed, he couldn't always stop to help me."

Lisa's physician said that because of the lupus, Lisa having even one child was a miracle. Lisa is coming to terms with how her life is different from what she originally dreamed it would be.

"I'm turning forty-one. I let go of my career. I let go of my idea of what kind of family we would have. A woman is valid no matter how many children she has. I had goals when I was twenty. I had goals when I was thirty. Now I am wiping the slate clean. I want to be Rachel's mom to the fullest. I am catching up to God and what he planned for me. As Rachel's mom, I am still helping God create a child. I am still assisting in that miracle."

Glossary of Medical Terms

Advanced Maternal Age (AMA). A woman is AMA if she will be at least thirty-five years old at her estimated date of delivery. At thirty-five, her chance of having a baby with Down syndrome is equal to her chance of having a miscarriage associated with second trimester amniocentesis.

amniocentesis. A procedure in which a needle is inserted through the mother's abdomen into the uterus to collect a sample of the amniotic fluid surrounding the baby. This test is performed between fifteen and twenty weeks. It has a miscarriage rate of 0.5 percent and a complication rate of 1 to 2 percent for vaginal bleeding or leakage of amniotic fluid.

amniotic fluid level. Amniotic fluid surrounds an unborn baby throughout pregnancy. Excessively high or low levels of fluid may indicate problems such as gestational diabetes or placental problems for the mother or physical problems with the baby that require further evaluation—and possibly an early delivery.

assisted reproductive technology (ART). A general term referring to methods used to achieve pregnancy by artificial or partially artificial means. It includes taking medications to induce ovulation, in vitro fertilization, and other techniques.

autoimmune disease. An immunological disease caused by the immune system attacking the body's own organs or tissues.

Clomiphene Citrate (Clomid) Challenge Test (CCCT). Clomid is the drug most widely used — and often the first used — to induce ovulation. The Challenge Test utilizes Clomid to assess "ovarian reserve." Ovarian reserve is a measure of the quality of the eggs remaining in a woman's ovaries. FSH levels are measured both before and after a woman takes Clomid for five days. Abnormal levels — either before or after — suggest a woman will respond poorly to ovulation induction.

Down syndrome. A congenital condition characterized by moderate to severe mental retardation; slanting eyes; a broad, short skull; and broad hands with short fingers. Also called trisomy 21.

ectopic pregnancy. Occurs when the fertilized ovum is implanted in any tissue other than the uterine wall. Most ectopic pregnancies occur in the fallopian tube (so-called tubal pregnancies), but implantation can occur in the cervix, ovaries, or abdominal cavity.

endometriosis. A medical condition where the tissue lining the uterus is found outside the uterus, typically affecting other organs in the pelvis. The condition can lead to serious health problems, primarily pain and infertility.

epidural. A local anesthetic delivered through a catheter in the small of the back, just outside the spinal canal. It allows most women to fully participate in the birth experience while relieving most, if not all, of the labor pains.

folic acid. A water-soluble vitamin in the B complex group. It works along with vitamin B-12 and vitamin C to help the body digest and utilize proteins. It also helps with tissue growth and cell production.

Follicle Stimulating Hormone (FSH). The hormone responsible for stimulating the follicles in the ovaries to mature. Evaluation of infertility may include checking FSH levels (a blood test) to see if a woman has adequate hormone amounts. Abnormal levels — either before or after testing — suggest a woman will respond poorly to ovulation induction.

genetic testing. Involves examining a person's DNA — taken from cells in a sample of blood or occasionally from other body fluids or tissues—for some anomaly that flags a disease or disorder. The DNA change can be relatively large, such as a missing or added piece of a chromosome, or even an entire chromosome, that is visible under a microscope. Or it can be extremely small, as little as one extra, missing, or altered chemical base.

gestational age. The time measured from the first day of the woman's last menstrual cycle to the current date, measured in weeks. A pregnancy of normal gestation is approximately forty weeks, with a normal range of thirty-eight to forty-two weeks.

gestational diabetes. Gestational diabetes is a type of diabetes that starts during pregnancy. If you have diabetes, your body isn't able to use the sugar (glucose) in your blood as well as it should, so the level of sugar in your blood becomes higher than normal. Gestational diabetes affects about 4 percent of all pregnant women. It usually begins in the fifth or sixth month of pregnancy (between the twenty-fourth and twenty-eighth weeks). Most often, gestational diabetes goes away after the baby is born. However, a woman who develops gestational diabetes is more likely to develop type 2 diabetes later in life.

gingivitis. Inflamed gums due to bacterial plaque building up on teeth.

human chorionic gonadotropin (HCG). A hormone produced by the embryo soon after conception and later by part of the placenta.

high-risk pregnancy. There is no formal or universally accepted definition of a "high-risk" pregnancy. Generally, however, a high-risk pregnancy involves at least one of the following: the woman or baby is more likely to become ill or die than usual, or complications before or after delivery are more likely to occur than usual. Certain conditions or characteristics, called risk factors, make a pregnancy high risk. Doctors identify these factors and use a scoring system to determine the degree of risk for a particular woman.

infertility. Medical practitioners define infertility as one year of unprotected sexual relations without conception.

intrauterine insemination (IUI). A medical procedure to insert the father's sperm into the mother's uterus. This is done to overcome possible cervical factors that would impede or kill a man's sperm.

in vitro fertilization (IVF). Fertilizing a woman's egg outside her body, i.e., within a laboratory. The fertilized egg is then transplanted into the woman's uterus.

Kegel exercise. Repetitive contractions by a woman of the muscles that are used to stop the urinary flow in urination in order to increase the tone of the pubococcygeal muscle, especially to control incontinence or to enhance sexual responsiveness during intercourse.

menopause. The natural cessation of menstruation occurring usually between the ages of forty-five and fifty-five. The average age of menopause is fifty-one to fifty-two.

neural tube. The structure in a developing embryo that gives rise to the brain and spinal cord.

neural tube defects. Any of various congenital defects, such as anencephaly and spina bifida, caused by incomplete closure of the neural tube during the early stages of embryonic development.

nuchal translucency. Swelling just under the skin at the back of the fetal neck. If the fetus has a greater than normal amount of swelling at the back of the neck, the likelihood is higher that the baby will have chromosomal abnormalities such as Down syndrome.

perimenopause. The period around the onset of menopause that is often marked by various physical signs, such as hot flashes and menstrual irregularity.

periodontal disease. Advanced gum disease involving loss of bone and teeth and gum abscesses.

pitocin. Synthetic form of oxytocin, a hormone produced by the pituitary gland. A maternal care provider may use pitocin to induce labor or to cause the uterus to contract after a delivery.

postpartum blues. A normal phenomenon that occurs in 70 percent of postpartum women. Symptoms last for ten to fourteen days and include weeping, irritability, restlessness, insomnia, and headaches.

postpartum depression. When "the blues" extend longer than fourteen days, they are considered postpartum depression. One in five postpartum women experiences postpartum depression. It can occur up to a year after a woman gives birth.

postpartum psychosis. A more serious condition that occurs in 0.1 percent of postpartum women, usually those with a personal history or family history of psychosis. Symptoms include schizophrenia, paranoia, and suicidal thoughts and can occur within days of giving birth or up to several months later.

preeclampsia. A serious condition developing in late pregnancy that is characterized by a sudden rise in blood pressure, excessive weight gain, generalized edema, proteinuria, severe headache, and visual disturbances and that may result in seizures (also known as eclampsia) if untreated.

spina bifida. A congenital defect of the spinal column that usually involves a protrusion of the spinal cord or its surrounding membranes.

ultrasound. A level one or basic ultrasound is a routine exam (lasting fifteen to twenty minutes) to determine pregnancy dates and location of the placenta and to check for birth defects. A level two or targeted ultrasound is a longer exam (thirty minutes to several hours) that typically uses more advanced ultrasound equipment to further investigate a fetal abnormality. A three-dimensional ultrasound is sometimes used during a targeted exam.

uterine polyp. Very common small growths dangling in the cavity of the womb. They can interfere with conception or implantation of an ovum.

Postpartum Depression Quiz

If you have been feeling "the blues" since having a baby, you may be at risk of developing postpartum depression. This quiz is designed to help you identify your feelings. Mark the answer that comes closest to how you have felt in the past seven days.

I am unable to laugh and see the funny side of things.	YES	NO
I cannot look forward to things with enjoyment.	YES	NO
I blame myself unnecessarily when things go wrong.	YES	NO
I am anxious or worried for no good reason.	YES	NO
I feel scared or panicky for no good reason.	YES	NO
Things have been getting on top of me.	YES	NO
I have been so unhappy that I have had difficulty sleeping.	YES	NO
I feel sad or miserable.	YES	NO

I have been so unhappy that I have been crying.   YES   NO
The thought of harming myself has occurred to me.   YES   NO

If you answered four or more of these with a "Yes," please tell your medical care provider.

Adapted from the Edinburgh Postnatal Depression
Scale (EPDS) and www.pvhs.org

About MOPS

You take care of your children, Mom. Who takes care of you? MOPS International (Mothers of Preschoolers) encourages, equips, and develops mothers of preschoolers to be the best moms they can be.

MOPS is dedicated to the message that "mothering matters" and understands that moms of young children need encouragement during these critical and formative years. Chartered MOPS groups meet in approximately 4,000 churches and Christian ministries throughout the United States and 24 other countries. Each MOPS group helps mothers find friendship and acceptance, provides opportunities for women to develop and practice leadership skills in a group, and promotes spiritual growth. MOPS groups are chartered ministries of local churches and meet at a variety of times and locations: daytime, evenings, and on weekends; in churches, homes, and workplaces.

The MOPPETS program offers a loving, learning experience for children while their moms attend MOPS. Other quality MOPS resources include *MOMSense* magazine, MOPS books available at www.MOPShop.org, website forums, and events.

With 14.3 million mothers of preschoolers in the United States alone, many moms can't attend a MOPS group. However, these moms still need the mothering support that MOPS International can offer! For a small registration fee, any mother of a preschooler can join the MOPS International Membership and receive *MOMSense* magazine (6 times a year), a weekly MOM-E-Mail of encouragement, and other valuable benefits.

Get Connected!
www.MOPS.org

Beth K. Vogt is a writer whose work has appeared in *Discipleship Journal*, *MOMSense*, and Crosswalk.com. She lives in Colorado Springs, Colorado, with her family.

Gentle, practical advice on how to make time for what matters most. Includes "breathing" exercises.

A deep breath for your soul, incorporating spiritual disciplines into your everyday life.

Mom-to-mom humor, encouragement, and practical advice on the crazy world of preschoolers.

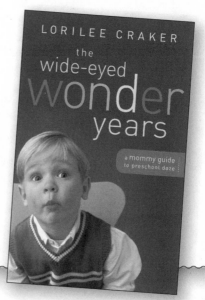

...because mothering matters
www.MOPS.org

ℜ Revell
www.revellbooks.com